SUBLIMINAL LEARNING

AN ECLECTIC APPROACH

BY ELDON TAYLOR, Ph.D.

WITH FOREWORD BY
ROBERT L. YOUNGBLOOD, M.D.

Box 7116
Salt Lake City
Utah 84107

83625

To my children

TABLE OF CONTENTS

FOREWORD

by ROBERT L. YOUNGBLOOD, M.D.

Dr. Robert L. Youngblood, a member of the board of advisers to Progressive Awareness Research, is a board certified plastic surgeon who has been in practice for more than twenty years. Dr. Youngblood trained at the Medical College of Georgia after obtaining an AB degree at Emory University in Atlanta. He went on to complete a general surgery residency at the Medical College of Georgia and a plastic surgery residency at the University of Utah Medical Center and LDS Hospital.

He is involved in many humanitarian efforts. His lifetime work as a surgeon and his longtime interest in human interpersonal transactions and self-imposed emotional limitations led him to a study of subliminal communication and its unquestioned value not only in the treatment of emotional and physical distress but also in the near limitless empowerment of human potential.

Dr. Youngblood has long understood the relationship that exists between the mind and the body and the ability of the subconscious to play an integral part in the healing process as well as to help in maintaining mental, physical, and emotional health.

As old paradigms evolve into (or abruptly change into) the new, resistance to the change is always greatest from the "established" representatives of "established" institutions and disciplines. It is no less so with the study and development of subliminal communication than with astronomy's declaration that Earth is not the axis of the universe, Semmelweis's pronouncement of the cause and prevention of puerperal fever, Lister's carbolic acid, "antiseptic" surgery techniques, or Freud's discovering and delving into the subconscious mind. Fortunately, man's evolution of consciousness has carried us beyond Rome's threat of thumbscrews and racking, the house imprisonment of Galileo, and the John Calvin mentality that executed Sevelius for daring to accurately record the human cardiovascular anatomy.

Ignorance, whether found in science, socioeconomics, or religion, may give rise to diverse kinds of controversy and conflict. Ignorance, though, is an invalid reason for impeding the development of important, even vital, processes and procedures, and must ultimately yield to the quest of those who step forward to champion their theories.

How important is subliminal communication?

The impossibility of "perfect" parenting coupled with our imperfect social environment assures that virtually everyone will spend a large portion of youth and early adulthood suffering from a surplus of inner negativity. The negativity that we associate with our inner self, our parents, our children, and others leaves us negatively charged and in need of positive reconstruction that will allow self-acceptance, the effective conduct of daily activity, and the optimal release of love and creativity.

Mind and body function are inseparable because of the powerful feedback that the one has on the other. Indeed, virtually every body component is or can be controlled by the mind, down to and including cellular function and response, and it can be done more powerfully and directly by the subconscious than by conscious effort.

In medicine, by far the most important element of healing is the patient's belief, attitude, and cooperation. In other words, the key is the patient's mental state. No quantity or quality of drugs, surgery, or other treatment can overcome disease in a totally negative patient. Positive mental attitude is essential for optimal therapeutic outcome. A method, instrument, substance, or other modality that has the potential of accomplishing that result is worthy of our most careful investigation and evaluation.

Experience shapes and changes our perspective, perspective affects belief, and belief filters our perception of our experiences. The complexity of the mind/brain/nerve/body/environment bio-lab-loop complicates the accurate measurement and evaluation of mind function. And yet, we live in a socio-scientific community in which only that which is measurable and repeatable is true. Since every person has a different body/mind bio-lab-loop, it is difficult and sometimes impossible to reproduce "measurements" and make valid comparisons between individuals or between groups. This is the enigma of the mind-function, and more especially of the researcher into the subconscious.

With his postgraduate background in science, pastoral psychology, and comparative religion, and with twelve years experience in criminology, Dr. Eldon Taylor is uniquely qualified to lead us into further exploration of subliminal perception and its effect on the subconscious mind. His contributions to this science-technology have been, and continue to be, impressive. He has taken a great step forward in presenting to us a clearer picture of our evolving consciousness. In *Subliminal Learning* he provides models for understanding the subception process together with overwhelming evidence of the efficacy of appropriate subliminal stimuli.

ABOUT THE AUTHOR

Dr. Eldon Taylor is an internationally recognized authority on subliminal communication and was a practicing criminologist specializing in forensic hypnosis and the detection of deception for twelve years. His work in the area of subliminal communication was featured in the *Omni Audio Experience* and has been reported in numerous articles in national print publications and on television and radio. He has written dozens of articles and books, recorded hundreds of audiocassettes, and given numerous television and radio interviews. He has earned multiple doctorates and has received many awards. His vita may be found in the *International Who's Who of Intellectuals*, published in Cambridge, England, together with several other prestigious biographical publications. Dr. Taylor founded Progressive Awareness Research, Inc., and originated the first subliminal research with incarcerated persons.

Books by Eldon Taylor, Ph.D., available from this publisher are:
> *Subliminal Communication*
> *Subliminal Technology*
> *Simple Things and Simple Thoughts*
> *The Little Black Book*
> *Exclusively Fabricated Illusions*

PREFACE

The self-responsible is the self-empowered. —Eldon Taylor

The original purpose of this work was, and to some extent still is, to disseminate the large body of data that has accumulated over the years in support of subliminal perception. Assembling this data while incorporating the dynamic of continuing research has taken years. During the evolution of my own learning, particularly that related to this project, I have made two significant discoveries. The first is simply that I cannot expect to assemble in one book all there is to know about subliminal communication or technology. At some point, assembling the material and reviewing the literature must end and the writing must begin. Sometimes I laugh at myself, for I am reminded of a saying that I have known for years: Only a fool claims to learn or do all things.

Thus I do not hold out this work as the "definitive" anything. Instead, it is intended to be a collection of materials that I have reviewed and discovered in my own learning curve as I reach to understand one aspect of the ultimate frontier—the human mind.

My second realization is implicit in the first. The study of subliminal communication is the study of the human condition. That is, to measure the effect of stimuli presupposes the background or reaction scenario known as behavior. The contemporary tradition of science calls for the distinguishing of one from the other, but this is never truly possible. Whether the study is of quantum mechanics or neuroscience, the process of the human condition with its attending perceptual lenses and behavioral propensities is the only "out there" something ever being studied. The experimenter and the experiment are so intricately interrelated that any distinction becomes no more meaningful than that of a cup of water taken from the sea.

Nevertheless, as Professor Bill Roe once stated in a letter to me, "The body of knowledge and techniques we call 'Science' is an information cornucopia which can be most supportive and nurturing when attempting the development and advancement of 'subliminal learning' concepts and technology. Remembering that yesterday's alchemy is today's quantum physics, psychology suggests great possibilities for the formalization and acceptance of tomorrow's 'subliminal science'." (Roe, 1988).

Given the pluralistic perspective for most educated people regarding knowledge and the manner in which they tend to structure learning according to their particular cognitive development (Norcross, 1970), perhaps an ecletic integration of science as a flexible and dynamic position on a given learning curve, relative to discipline, and science as the "hard" and final authority would indeed be more representative of what science is and has always been.

From the perspective of this experimenter/experiment, one issue repeatedly revealed itself during this work as if to say, "Ah, but for me the human potential would be realized," "Ah, but for me, the self-alienation that has become a natural product of being human would cease to be," "Ah, but for me, the wasteland of disease would blossom into the land of milk and honey," "Ah, but for me, the fear of rejection (itself only an illusion), the world would discover that there must be a mental dysfunction before there exists a physical disease." Therefore *Subliminal Learning* proposes to be not just a text on subliminal communication and technology, but also something of a treatise on self-responsibility. All behavior is behavior of choice, even if it is painful, resistive, and subliminally chosen.

With deference to the scientific method and its invaluable orientation toward information gathering and assessment and yet with a strong desire to reach as large an audience as possible, a decision had to be made regarding the technical level of communication in this volume. A middle ground was therefore decided upon. For the scholar, a complete bibliography and additional reading list is included. Some of the studies cited have multiple findings, not all of which have been included. I truly hope each reader will find the material that follows to be worthwhile and self-empowering.

ACKNOWLEDGMENTS

The thousands of hours of research, planning, writing, and miscellanea behind this book deeply indebt me to a number of people who in some way helped make it possible.

Many who have gone before me have provided the foundations for my learning, and I extend my gratitude to all of these people. A special acknowledgment is due Catherine Sanders, who worked hundreds of hours as my research assistant, and to the board of advisers of Progressive Awareness Research, Inc., who counseled and supported me in both the research and the writing of this work. The advisers are, alphabetically:

Roy Bey, B.S.
William Guillory, Ph.D
Lee Liston, B.S., S.S.W.
Linda Liston, M.S., S.S.W.
Jerry Poulson, M.D.
Laura Preece, A.A.S.
Catherine Sanders, B.S.
Jim Seidel, Ph.D.
Robert Youngblood, M.D.

I am also deeply indebted to members of the Mind Mint system who shared with me their experiences, data, and mailing lists (making it possible to mail self-appraisal questionnaires to thousands of users). Thanks to Ben, Bob, Candace, Carol, Cat, Dorothy, Jan, John, Juanita, Judy, Kim, Kris, Lee, Lon, Michelle, Mike, Rebecca, Rob, Sandy, Tracy, and Wayne.

Many references to published material appear in the work that follows and, while acknowledgment is due to all, I wish to extend special thanks to William Guillory, Ph.D., and Julian Jaynes, Ph.D., and to *Brain/Mind Bulletin* and Shambhala Publications for permission to quote their works extensively.

Special thanks is also due to Laura Preece, who assisted in gathering and compiling clinical data, organizing and writing case reports, and proofreading and assisting in the editing process.

A number of manuscripts were sent to various professionals for their comments and criticism. Many valuable contributions to this work were so obtained and to all who assisted in this way—thank you. A very special expression of gratitude in this regard is due Professor Roe of Phoenix College.

Finally, but not least by any means, acknowledgment is due to Suzanne, Lori, Eileen, Norma, and Mary Ann, who took my handwritten pages and prepared and edited them for publication, and to Warren Archer, who took the painting *Listening for Voices* by the talented artist Clayton Anderson and incorporated copy, color, and layout for the cover design.

CHAPTER ONE

THE CONTROVERSY ABOUT SUBLIMINALS

*Small minds condemn what they do
not understand. —Richard Sutphen*

"IT DOESN'T WORK, BUT IT IS DANGEROUS"

To say that subliminal communication is controversial is a gross understatement. The public views subliminal technology ambivalently at best. Many psychologists assert that there just isn't any evidence that it works, but stay away from it—it is dangerous! That proposition seems absurd to me. How can something not perceived be perceived as dangerous?

A telephone survey published in the *Journal of Advertising* in 1983 revealed that of 209 subjects, 81 percent had some knowledge of subliminal advertising, and an equal percentage of those with some knowledge believed that it was being used in advertising to manipulate consumers. By a margin of two to one, subjects believed this usage was both harmful and unethical. Two other conclusions may be drawn from the responses of the subjects:

1

1. Respondents believe subliminal advertising is widespread despite their inability to strongly associate a particular spokesperson with subliminal advertising.
2. The individual most likely to have heard of subliminal communication is white, well-educated, with an income in excess of twenty thousand dollars per year. (Zanot, Pincus, Lamp, 1983.)

In another telephone survey conducted by Block and Vanden Bergh of Michigan State University, 330 adults were contacted to determine attitudes toward subliminal self-help products. This study revealed that consumers were skeptical of subliminal self-improvement products and were also concerned about being influenced to do something they did not wish to do. Respondents disclosed different attitudes toward subliminal technology in advertising than toward subliminals in other uses. The survey also found that:

1. Those most aware and concerned about subliminal advertising tended to be white, well-educated, and affluent.
2. Those most favorable to subliminal technology in self-improvement products were less educated and experiencing some family problems. (Block, Vanden Bergh, 1985.)

To me, this "public" attitude seems ridiculous. If something works (as subliminals in advertising), then it works. How it can *not* work and still be dangerous is an obvious error in thinking.

Why does such an obvious flaw in reasoning go unnoticed? Perhaps because as victims we fear the world—*they* might coerce or manipulate us. But if we accept that we might use subliminal technology for self-improvement, we must recognize that implicit in this acceptance is the notion that *we* somehow can learn to help ourselves and therefore have no one to blame except ourselves for our failures and weaknesses. I have been asked on many occasions why there is such a disparity between the thinking of the professional and the thinking of the lay person regarding subliminal technology. This is the only experientially valid reasoning I have been able to discern.

It has been suggested that the government was keeping subliminal technology a secret, a sort of Orwellian scheme designed to control the population, or that psychologists resisted subliminal learning, particularly self-help aids, because of their vested financial interests. Personally, I find neither of these proposals credible, although various governments have conducted studies and experimentation with subliminal communication.

I am inclined to believe that fear and ignorance are the issues underpinning most of the controversy over subliminal communication. The ignorance is regarding the research and data presently assembled, and the fear arises from the implicit set, the acceptance of personal responsibility, which accompanies the subliminal communication paradigm.

The press has repeatedly juxtaposed two parties addressing the subliminal issue. One is usually a college instructor, the other an independent researcher, manufacturer, salesperson, or consumer. The college instructor will usually oppose the use of subliminal uses as something which does not work, has no valid science behind it, and is dangerous. The other person will offer in defense anecdotal evidence. My own experience with this has taught me that even when you provide the citations which I have done, for example, in the bibliography of this book, either the press does not know how to treat the subject and still have controversial copy or they elect simply to ignore it. (Perhaps they have their own fears.)

One such instance took place in *Insight* magazine's 14 September 1987 issue. The author of the article was provided with pounds of material from my office. Her lead sentence begins: "Though proof of their effectiveness is hard to come by. . . . " (P. 44.) The article goes on to state that although subliminal techniques are *not* allowed in advertising, they are netting profits in the tape industry because consumers are betting that subliminals work, "even if no one—including manufacturers—is quite sure how." (P. 45.)

Why bother to phone someone for information if you are not going to listen to what they say? Why ask for evidence if you then ignore the answer? These are just a couple of the questions that went through my mind when I saw the *Insight* article, which brings me to another question: Are they perpetuating the controversy for good copy?

A similar instance, but one involving even poorer journalistic responsibility, occurred with an interview I gave a Logan, Utah, newspaper reporter. The paper's staff writer quoted Dr. Elwin Nielson, associate professor of psychology at Utah State University, as stating that subliminal communication in self-help products was exploiting the consumer. "It's sad," Nielson is quoted as

3

saying, "They [consumers] are being exploited in the same way a con man exploits a widow out of a $3,000 nest egg for pie in the sky." When Nielson answered my corporate counsel's letter, he stated flatly that the journalist in question had misrepresented herself, taken few if any notes, and quoted him out of context.

What does all of this translate into as far as the public is concerned? More controversy! Once again, an appropriate question would be, why? Does the media deliberately desire to confuse the issue?

When Elaine Jarvik wrote a feature story on subliminal self-improvement, a fair balance between the antagonists and supporters was represented. Still, a rather subliminal joke found its way into the printed story. The article concluded with a testimony from Diana Steed, who reported a measurable increase in breast size as a result of listening to a subliminal audiocassette on breast enlargement. Steed went on to offer before and after pictures as proof. The article contains three bold letters, one in each column. They spell, in a mound configuration:

I

T   T

(See opposite page.)

Was this just an accident? Or perhaps someone's sense of humor? Is it also possible that it was done to attract readers or, in the alternative, to mock the copy? In this same article a professor from the University of Utah made the classic comment that it doesn't work and besides, it's dangerous—stay away from it!

Bob Tripe reports in a United Press International release that psychologist Thomas Wilkinson of Grand Rapids had two or three patients using the tapes. In juxtaposition to Wilkinson was psychologist Ivan Ross of Minneapolis. Ross is quoted as asserting that the use of subliminal communication was "a ridiculous subject matter" and that "it has no practical value."

THE EVIDENCE CONTROVERSY

In this same piece Tripe quotes psychologist Joseph Smith as stating, "The body of scientific evidence shows there's no substance to them [subliminals]." This I have heard many times, and I

DESERET NEWS

Living • Dear Abby
Meaningful Marriage • TV
Comics • Theater

Living

Today

Thursday, January 29, 1987

'Silent' voices: Can subliminal tapes change your life?

By Elaine Jarvik
Deseret News staff writer

Charlie McCusker had some warts on his feet. Painful and perverse, they were removed by various medical methods involving acid and frozen gas, only to return again and again. Then McCusker began listening to a tape produced by a company called Potentials Unlimited. He listened to the tape once a day for 10 days, at which point, he says, the warts simply faded away.

Warts are known for their capriciousness, here one day and sometimes spontaneously gone the next. But McCusker is certain that his warts' disappearance was not mere coincidence.

McCusker, who is a doctoral candidate in educational psychology at the University of Utah, listened to the "Removal of Warts" tape for 30 minutes a day, usually at bedtime.

These are "subliminal tapes." Although they do contain a message, the only thing the conscious mind hears is the sound of soothing guitar music and ocean waves. The message — which in Charlie's case included statements such as "your health is improving daily" — is designed to be picked up only by the subconscious.

One message at least is clear, however: Charlie McCusker is not alone. There are people all over the Salt Lake valley who at this very moment are listening to subliminal tapes in the hope of doing nearly everything from improving their tennis game to overcoming their fear of success.

There is a tape designed to cure insomnia and a tape to help you get by on less sleep. There is a tape for world peace and one for facial tics, for creative thinking and improved sex. Nearly every human hope and frailty is catalogued and confronted on the hundreds of subliminal tapes now on the market.

It looks like the ultimate therapy for busy people. No need to pay for weekly trips to the psychiatrist, to practice anything, think about anything, explore unpleasant memories, endure any pain.

But can subliminal messages really affect the way we feel and act?

"There is no evidence, no respectable evidence, that such a thing could work," argues Dr. William Johnston, professor of psychology at the University of Utah.

Dr. Eldon Taylor disagrees. Taylor is developmental advisor for the Mind Mint, a franchise of Salt Lake valley "cerebral emporiums" that sell subliminal tapes. He is also author of "Subliminal Communication: Emperor's Clothes or Panacea?," published last year by JAR (Just Another Reality), the parent company of the Mind Mint.

Subliminal communication, says Taylor, "is potentially the most powerful form of communication known to man."

THERE ARE COUNTLESS anecdotes: Anecdotes about weight loss, reductions in shoplifting, increases in energy, lowered blood pressure, even hair growth on balding men.

Judy Goddard, an interior designer, has bought more than 30 tapes, including one to improve sales and one to improve her children's study habits. She says both her sales and her children's grades have gone up.

Goddard also likes to play the "I Am Enthusiastic" tape when she throws a party. "It gets people talking," she says.

Arnold Stringham, co-owner of the Spencer and Stringham Real Estate Education Center, says he used to be an "8 to 12 Excedrin a day person" until he began to listen to a tape called "Headache Relief."

What the tape does, says Stringham, is "change a condition in your mind."

Mind over what's the matter with you is the key ingredient of subliminal self-help. The premise is that 1) through our minds we can affect our health and chronic behavior patterns, but 2) often our conscious minds reject this help, so 3) subliminal tapes get the proper messages to our subconscious minds and then we are free to make changes in the way we feel and act.

Because the messages are masked by music or "pink noise," the tapes can be played any time. Some people buy auto-reverse tape recorders, put them under their pillows and listen to the subliminal cassettes all night long.

The American public first heard about subliminal perception in 1956, when a New Jersey market researcher reported that he had flashed visual subliminal messages on the screen during the movie "Picnic." According to his claims, the messages "eat popcorn" and "drink Coca-Cola" were flashed over Kim Novak's face every five seconds for a fraction of a

(Reproduced by permission.)

second for six weeks — and this resulted in a 58 percent increase in popcorn sales and an 18 percent increase in Coke sales.

"Subliminal tapes bypass the conscious mind," explains Eldon Taylor. Taylor, who has a doctoral degree in pastoral psychology from the University of Metaphysics in Los Angeles, opened the first Mind Mint with his wife, Annette, in 1984. The franchise is now the largest direct dealer of subliminal programs in the country.

There are over 700 subliminal titles available. Taylor says his best sellers are the the 23rd Psalm and the "I'm Drug Free" tape which he wrote and now gives away free to parents. Taylor himself listens to the 23rd Psalm tape a lot. At his wife's request, he also began listening to a "Stop Smoking" tape and reports that, after 10 days, cigarettes tasted horrible. So he put the tape in his glove compartment and hasn't listened to it since, he says, taking a drag on yet another cigarette.

IN 1986, TAYLOR, Charlie McCusker and Lee Liston, a case worker at the Utah State Prison, did a study of subliminal tapes using 38 inmates at the young adult correctional facility at the prison. Some of the inmates listened to a subliminal tape that contained messages such as "I create my future" and "I like myself." Some inmates listened to a placebo tape, and others heard no tapes. All inmates were given the Thurstone Temperament Schedule test at the beginning and end of the three-month study.

The results, says Taylor, show that those inmates who listened to the subliminal tape scored higher in "stability" and "reflectivity" than the control group did.

Taylor admits that his study had limitations, including the fact that, by the end of the three months, most of the inmates had dropped out of the study.

Liston says he is excited about the possibilities of using subliminal tapes in prison rehabilitation. He and Taylor hope to do a new study in the maximum security facility this year.

With a grant from the Institute of Human Development in Ojai, Calif., Taylor also plans to do a study of the effect of subliminal tapes on breast enlargement. Unlike the prison study, which measures the somewhat fuzzy area of personality change, the breast enlargement study will measure the subliminals' effect in millimeters. Taylor will conduct the study with Salt Lake plastic surgeon Robert Youngblood.

This will be one of the few double blind studies of audio subliminal perception conducted to date. Although there are many anecdotes and some studies using experimental and control groups, there is apparently only one published double-blind study in which a placebo group is also used.

But, says Taylor, "the preponderance of evidence shows that it at least warrants further investigation."

U. of U. psychology professor William Johnston agrees with the need for more investigation, but can't find much evidence — other than anecdotes — that subliminal messages are even perceived by the subconscious.

Johnston, who authored an article on perception in the 1986 Annual Review of Psychology, says that his own research indicates that when even just a single word is masked with other noise such as music, the word is not registered by the subconscious.

But Eldon Taylor wonders, then, how you can explain the success he has had with this experiment: He repeats a three-digit number, on a subliminal tape, to a room full of people, then asks them to pick out the number from five three-digit alternatives. If he plays the tapes for 30 or 60 minutes, he says, 70 percent of the people pick the correct number.

On an anecdotal basis — stories about warts and blood pressure and better grades — success with subliminal tapes could be attributed to wishful thinking or the placebo effect.

Judy Goddard wonders, however, how this would explain why her husband lost 36 pounds when he didn't even know she was playing a weight loss tape.

Clearly, as Eldon Taylor says, "we have a lot more questions than answers." Taylor is confident that the tapes are beneficial and points to his refund policy as proof. "We say, if you have no beneficial gain (within 60 days), we'll refund your money, but out of tens of thousands of tapes sold, only a few have been returned."

TAYLOR RECOMMENDS tapes with simple, positive messages, so that the brain does not misconstrue them. A message such as "smoking will kill me" might, in fact, kill you, he says. He advises that people purchase tapes that include either a spoken version on the other side of the tape, or a written script. Whether the subliminal message is identical to the script (and isn't telling you something else, such as "Buy more tapes") has to be taken on faith.

According to Virgil Hayes, director of the Hypnotism Training Institute of Utah, several stores in the Salt Lake valley are using subliminal messages to curb shoplifting and employee theft. Hayes, who says he produced the tapes for these stores, said he could not divulge the names of the stores, but that the stores have noticed a decrease in both kinds of theft. There are currently no laws regulating the use of subliminal messages in public places.

Scientific proof about the effectiveness of subliminal tapes may be less than conclusive, but the public appears eager to plug in the cassettes and see what happens. At American Express headquarters on 2700 West, the employee health library now includes subliminal tapes on stress, weight loss and smoking. Most local bookstores carry at least a few tapes. Holladay dentist Leon Hendricksen sometimes uses tapes that subliminally tell his patients "You are relaxed. You are having a normal, happy experience."

"People like to believe things like that," says psychology professor Johnston about subliminal tapes. "We're always looking for easy ways out."

While Johnston and others scoff at the notion that voices you can't hear can change your life, Diana Steed has become a believer. For the last four months, Steed has been listening to a tape on breast enlargement and reports that the results are "amazing." And, she says, she has pictures to prove it.

ILLUSTRATION/ ROBERT HOYCE

have repeatedly asked for this "body" of evidence. None has been revealed. When I have asked those making such statements to name a study or give me an example, the retort goes something like this: "Well, what I mean is, there exists no evidence that demonstrates subliminals work." Is this what is meant by a "body of evidence"?

Over the past few years, especially since writing *Subliminal Communication*, I have interacted with thousands of people in seminars, workshops, and radio broadcasts. Not one opponent of subliminals has ever produced a "body" (let alone a finger or toe) of evidence. I have often suggested to professionals that they simply access their own university library computer files. Hundreds of times I have shared my experience of obtaining from the psychology and medical files at the University of Utah's Marriott Library several hundred references to scientific findings supporting the reality and efficacy of subliminal communication.

And the controversy heightens. John Lofflin reported in the *New York Times* in March 1988 that an estimated 250 million subliminal self-help tapes were sold in 1987. Lofflin mentions the findings of Howard Shevrin, a professor of psychology at the University of Michigan with thirty years of study in subliminal perception. Shevrin's findings indicate that subliminal messages relating to an internal conflict will produce unique, measurable brain patterns within a given subject. Some messages, however, may produce violent, bitter, or severe responses rather than solve the conflict. Nevertheless, Shevrin is quoted in the September 1988 issue of *Psychology Today* as asserting that claims by subliminal manufacturers regarding scientific evidence are a "scam."

In February 1987 the *National Enquirer* ran a story on hidden messages. Everyone I have asked to read the article believes that the way the article is written suggests that Jim Nelson actually spoke to me and to Wilson Key. In reality, he took his interview (at least my part) from my book *Subliminal Communication*. Although this article does not question the power of subliminal persuasion, its covert and manipulative use is emphasized. Wilson Key is quoted as stating that a number of police departments, including the San Francisco Police Department, are using subliminal programs in their interrogation rooms. (Nelson, 1988.)

6

THE REAL CONTROVERSY

Perhaps the real controversy occurs because of the covert and surreptitious uses allegedly made of subliminal technology. Whether the Orwellian syndrome or the self-responsible antithesis to the 1984 scenario, fear frustrates the issue by breeding sensational and controversial departures from pure fact-finding.

Recent headlines regarding the expanding subliminal self-help market and the ever-expanding use of subliminal technology has in many instances fanned the fire. In April 1987 *Building Supply and Home Centers* (formerly *Building Supply News*) proposed "high-tech hardware" to curb theft. Closed circuit television and subliminal suggestions represented this high-tech approach. (*Building Supply & Home Centers*, 1987.)

The Providence *Journal* reported that according to a study by the National Crime Prevention Council, sixteen billion dollars a year is shoplifted from retailers. The *Journal* went on to quote L. Connors, director of Shoplifters Anonymous, that where a subliminal deterrent has been installed, shoplifting has been reduced by 25 to 36 percent. (Providence *Journal*, 1986.)

The *Business Week Industrial Edition* has warned that Wall Street was using a visual medium to offer subliminal messages that could be unduly influential. Their source was an executive vice president of an advertising agency specializing in financial products. (*Business Week Industrial Edition*, 1986.)

According to International Resource Development of Norwalk, Connecticut, software has expanded to meet growing demand. Some of the new programs are designed to meet personal needs and consequently focus on diagnosing illness symptoms, dealing with exercise and nutritional issues, and facilitating behavior modification. "Some programs simply raise the user's awareness; others flash subliminal messages." (News release, 1985.)

Marketing News in June 1985 suggested using the subliminal effect on billboards in outdoor advertising. (*Marketing News*, 1985.) *Marketing Communications* reported that "subliminal projection techniques would probably work in TV advertising." They went on to state, "Recent psychological tests have shown the technique will elicit emotional reactions from viewers even though the actual

7

mental processes responsible for it are at the unconscious level."
(*Marketing Communications*, 1985.)

Proactive Systems of Portland, Oregon, is reported as offering
subliminal messaging systems to retailers. The article suggests that
Proactive's system technically is not subliminal, since messages
could be heard if "you were right next to the speaker" and therefore its use is not a violation of FCC regulations. (*Marketing
News*, 1985.)

Greentree Publishers in 1985 announced software that "flashes
subliminal messages on employees' VDTs" (video display terminals, more commonly known as CRTs—cathrode-ray terminals).
Any kind of message can be flashed upon the screen. (*Computer
Decisions*, 1985.)

New Life Institute in Santa Cruz, California, offers subliminal
software for the IBM PC that provides for user-chosen "subconscious suggestions." According to their news release, "In eight
hours at the computer, the user receives 28,800 suggestions flashed
at a subconscious rate." (News release, 1984.)

Stimutech in East Lansing, Michigan, which I understand is now
out of business, also had a device that puts subliminal content
onto the computer screen. "The Expando-Vision interfacing box
equipped with the proper program flashes an extremely short message on the screen once every 2.5 minutes. As a result, the subconscious becomes imprinted with messages that can bring about
changes in behavior," the company announcement asserted.
(*Merchandising*, 1983.)

Entertel of New York City has announced that they are "seek-
ing advertisers to slip short messages into its 'ambient video'
productions." Owner of Entertel, S. Young, admitted that this is
subliminal advertising but planned his first venture around advertising jeans in an "hourlong color montage of 'Fabulous Females,'
a video which shows women wiggling in bathing suits, shorts,
skirts, and now, jeans." (*Advertising Age*, 1985.)

According to *Women's Wear Daily*, the Allison Group re-
launched the Pier Auge skin treatment line by creating Pier Auge
Institutes that play subliminal tapes during their 1.5-hour facial.
(*Women's Wear Daily*, 1987.)

Environmental Video introduced a "subliminal persuasion
video" cassette that superimposes video messages on cassette tapes.
(*VideoNews*, 1983.)

Advertising Age reported that *New Woman* magazine "has developed what it calls 'subliminal synergism,' a technique whereby the dominant color or colors of a four-color ad page are picked up on the page opposite as a color-coded tint block behind a headline." (*Advertising Age*, 1982.)

ACADEMIC ADVERTISING

Where subliminal advertising is concerned, a paper by Eric Zanot and Lynda Maddox asserts that "the academic community ignores the subject of subliminal advertising." Further, a study they conducted to ascertain the degree to which subliminal communication is introduced into advertising-related courses in colleges and universities by professors of those courses derived four significant conclusions:

1. These professors are fully cognizant of the concept;
2. Although it is discussed in a wide variety of classes, little class time is devoted to subliminal advertising;
3. Subliminal advertising is also discussed in a variety of other departments;
4. Educators in advertising or marketing departments teach that it is seldom or never used. (Zanot, Maddox, 1983.)

According to a study conducted by Cuperfain and Clarke, "academic marketers may have been too quick to discount the ability of subliminal presentations to affect consumer decision making." (Implications for advertising and hemispheric specialization studies are noted.) (Cuperfain, Clarke, 1985.)

In 1977, R. Zamora of Florida, a fifteen-year-old boy, offered as his defense to a first-degree murder charge an insanity plea based upon "involuntary subliminal TV intoxication." (*Broadcasting*, 1977.)

Heavy metal groups have long been charged with using satanic, sexual, and drug-related subliminal messages in their recordings. Ozzy Osbourne's "Suicide Solution" cut was unmasked by Stephen Williamson of Oregon. Williamson is the director of the Institute for Bio-Acoustics Research. Williamson was hired by the attorney for a California family who were suing, alleging that "Osbourne's death-obsessed lyrics, particularly the 'masked' passage" had contributed to the suicide of their nineteen-year-old son. A Los Angeles

9

Superior Court judge dismissed the lawsuit on the basis of constitutionally protected free speech. (Ruben, 1987.)

I was once asked to use a heavy metal recording in a subliminal program for a particular football team. When I amplified the track through a parametric equalizer, verbal content not formerly audible became obvious. Later, because the football team was very successful (and we did not use this soundtrack), the story came out in the media. The South Ogden Police Department contacted me for the details and disclosed that they had an operational public education program targeting "subliminal messages sometimes integrated into the music itself to influence people." Additionally, the agency possessed equipment with the capability "of separating tracks" to find subliminal content. (South Ogden Police Department, 1987.)

In my book *Subliminal Communication*, I discuss speaking with a sound engineer who *was* the person mixing subliminal messages into popular music at the request of many prominent groups and artists. According to this person, he stopped when the effects of the messages became observable in the music fans' behavior.

In the November 1985 issue of *American Psychologist*, John Vokey and J. Read assert that "backmasking," the most common heavy metal subliminal mixing technique, is "a function more of active construction on the part of the perceiver than of the existence of the messages themselves." (Vokey, Read, 1985.)

In Canada use of subliminal communication is not as highly controversial. A Canadian radio station, CIME-FM of Ste. Therese, Quebec, is broadcasting anti mosquito frequencies in their music programming. "The station also broadcasts subliminal relaxation messages in the evening and subliminal energizing messages in the morning." (*Wall Street Journal*, 1985.)

In January 1987 the Canadian Radio-Television and Telecommunications Commission decided they would no longer prohibit subliminal advertising "but has asked the industry to come up with its own guidelines." (*Marketing*, 1987.)

The University of Montreal used a radio station to broadcast music in which subliminal health and relaxation messages had been mixed. A survey of one hundred listeners showed that most used the programming to decrease tension and improve sleep. (Borgeat, Chaloult, 1985.)

10

Subliminal Training

Subliminal training techniques go back at least to what Ohio State University termed "minimal perception." The technique was developed in the Second World War to train United States Navy gunners. "Researchers flashed silhouettes of enemy aircraft on a screen for gunners to identify. At exposures of 1/100th of a second, gunners were trained to identify more than 2,000 silhouettes at one sitting without a mistake." (Barenklau, 1981.)

Since this early military use, rumors have proliferated regarding brainwashing methods as well as training procedures that incorporate subliminal technology. An associate of mine, Dr. Carl Schleicher of Mankind Research Unlimited, Inc., and the Accelerated Learning Institute, both of Silver Spring, Maryland, incorporates sophisticated subliminal embeds in flash cards used to teach foreign languages to government personnel. Schleicher's work is in part an outgrowth of the genius of the Bulgarian psychiatrist Dr. Georgi Lazanov, who successfully taught children foreign languages at the incredible rate of up to one thousand words per day. According to Schleicher, United States government, academic, and corporate research has documented the efficacy of the subliminal-embed method.

Under a federal grant Dr. Schleicher successfully trained blind people to become computer operators. The Center of Preventive Therapy and Rehabilitation, where Schleicher is director, successfully accomplished the training using several techniques, including subliminal cues and creative imagery.

I have received many letters accusing governments, churches, and individuals of using subliminal technology in one way or another to exercise a controlling influence on people. Many times I have been asked about possibilities of microwave and radio transmissions. Of course, broadcasting a subliminal message in that manner is possible. Perhaps that is why Cuba broadcasts radio programming underneath United States stations, and maybe that is why the FCC orders certain United States stations down from time to time—not to determine whether the practice continues but rather to examine the content, for when the United States station is down, the Cuban program comes in loud and clear.

11

Bioacoustical studies have demonstrated that frequencies can affect organisms, and these frequencies, if not subliminal by their range, certainly can be broadcast subliminally.

In principle, every artifact of our world has a good and a bad potential. When we are all through with the paranoia over subliminals, perhaps we can move beyond the controversy over their existence to a discussion of their use and technical nuances.

CHAPTER TWO

ACCOMMODATING SUBLIMINAL COMMUNICATION

Science is an information cornucopia which can nurture and support the development and advancement of "subliminal learning" concepts and technology.—From Bill Roe

In *Handbook of Eclectic Psychotherapy*, John Norcross conceptualizes three developmental stages in learning (accepting) new information: "In the first of three developmental stages in learning new information, one perceives or experiences a global whole, with no clear distinctions among component parts. Unsophisticated laypersons and undergraduates probably fall into this category.

"In the second stage, one perceives or experiences differentiation of the whole into parts, with a more precise and distinct perspective of components within the whole. However, one no longer has a perspective on the whole, and subsequently loses the 'big

13

picture.' Most psychotherapy courses, textbooks, and formally educated practitioners fall into this category.

"In the third stage, the differentiated parts are organized and
integrated into the whole at a higher level. Here, the unity and
complexity of psychotherapy are appreciated. Few psychothera-
pists have successfully reached this summit, but many more are
scaling the slope." (Norcross, 1986.)

The second of these stages is characterized as dualistic, according to Norcross, who refers to the work of Prochaska. Dualistic
psycho-therapists believe that they possess the "revealed truth."
Norcross states that "they are the true believers among us who
think that one therapy system is correct and all others are errone-
ous. These dualistic therapists, found in all orientations, are the
result not of the structure of the systems in which they believe,
but rather the structure of their own intellects." (Ibid.) It is toward
the dualistic, second-stage expert that energetic argument has occasionally been directed. Ample room exists to integrate subliminal
communication with the present psychotherapeutic procedure of
preference, and more than sufficient evidence to suggest that at
the very least and regardless of technique bias on the part of the
therapist, subliminal information processing will indeed enhance
patient motivation and expectation. No clear statistical evidence
exists to demonstrate the superior efficacy of one therapy approach
over another (e.g., psychoanalytic vs. Rogerian vs. Neo-Freudian,
etc.). Yet the evidence does favor consensus regarding the differential effectiveness of therapies: the most meaningful difference
in therapy outcome is client dependent, determined by such factors as motivation and willingness to assume responsibility. (Ibid.)

One of the many advantages to subliminal communication as
an ancillary aid in therapy is its generally supportive and motivational characteristics, all of which will be more completely discussed later. If a subliminal program did no more than assist
a client in this regard, then obviously subliminal communication would be a significant contribution to the therapeutic paradigm. In actuality, as will be seen, subliminal information processing promises to provide client and therapist much more
than motivation: it promises to help in building esteem, engaging
counterproductive defense mechanisms at their origins, even
confronting self-destructive adaptations in a sort of subliminal
workshop.

CHAPTER THREE

What You Perceive That You Don't

The most complicated achievements of thought are possible without the assistance of consciousness.
—Sigmund Freud

Introduction

The human can and does effectively sense, perceive, and act on undetected stimuli. In fact, as sophisticated sensing devices go, the human is in many ways superior to modern equipment marvels. It has long been recognized that patterns of perception, such as those formalized under the general heading of parapsychology, have yet to be fully integrated into the overall information processing model of the human condition. The fact is that the human is extremely sensitive to a variety of stimuli that go consciously unrecognized. The brain does respond to information that the mind is oblivious to. The capacity of the brain to process information does not require or even necessarily include conscious attention

15

or representation. More than sufficient research supports the plain fact that whether it is in learning, memory, perception, attention, or emotion, these processes can and do occur without conscious involvement. (Dixon, 1981.)

Some theorists assert that cognitive systems (consciousness) evolved for the gratification of needs. As such, "perception, memory and thinking are primarily concerned with detecting, analysing, storing and responding to those features of the environment which are relevant to survival." (Ibid.)

SUBLIMINAL MECHANICS

I have been asked repeatedly to explain how it is possible to perceive something that is not perceived. I asked this question myself when I first became aware of subliminal stimulation. In fact, my earliest inquiries into subliminal stimuli were from the viewpoint of the proverbial doubting Thomas and devil's advocate. As a practicing criminologist administering lie detection tests daily, I wanted to believe it was possible, if only for selfish reasons. If verbal stimulus presented below the threshold of awareness could indeed be perceived, I reasoned that this same verbal stimulus could be presented in such a way as to produce a physiological response. After all, the process of lie detection testing involves producing measurable physiological responses following appropriate psychological stimuli. In a sense, lie detection equipment is only sophisticated biofeedback instrumentation. I thus theorized that appropriate subliminal stimuli could minimize situational stress for the truthful while increasing physiological responses during the practice of deception.

I experimented with this theory while researching subliminal technology years ago and satisfied myself and my colleagues that in fact the theory worked. I am aware of deception detection examiners that to this day employ subliminal stimulation in lie detection testing.

There is no simple answer to the question regarding the perception of that which went unperceived. The study of perception, its process and mechanisms, has long occupied philosophers, theologians, and psychologists. Consciousness itself is not fully

16

understood, let alone one of its artifacts: perception. What is consciousness without an object? What is perception without recognition? Is there really such a thing as stimulus-independent mentation? When is an unconscious experience a stimulation? Is it possible to be unconscious of consciousness? When is a subconscious learning made conscious? Is it true that the conscious mind derives its pride from the vaster storehouse of knowledge existing in the subconscious? Indeed, can the conscious mind only guess at what exists in the subconscious while the subconscious knows all that is in the conscious mind? Does the subconscious mind even provide the conscious with guesses as to what is really contained in the subconscious or unconscious regions of the mind?

Most of the controversy over subliminal communication among professionals has arisen out of definitional differences. (Wolman, 1973.) Dozens of definitions of *unconscious* and *perception* have complicated the issue. Without meaningful reference points on these two critical constructs, terms such as *awareness, subliminal*, and *subception* become words with little meaning or no more meaning than pure nonsense syllables. In *Handbook of General Psychology*, edited by Benjamin B. Wolman, Wolman states:

> It seems, then, as in the related area of perceptual defense, that much of the controversy in this area [subliminal research] stems from differing theoretical and experimental predilections of different researchers. This in turn leads to different definitions of the terms "subliminal" and "awareness," as well as to different experimental methods, which, in turn, make it difficult to compare studies using different stimuli; different response measures, and different threshold procedures. (1973.)

In an attempt to minimize confusion, I have opted to adopt popular terms and to provide a general working definition. (See chapter 4.) So, back to the original question: how is it possible to perceive what we do not perceive, indeed *register* much stimuli that goes *unrecognized*? What is really being treated at large as subliminal perception is in fact unrecognized or nonrecognized stimuli registering at some level below the threshold of distinguishability or recognition. A little history and some expounding of the

17

mechanics behind the production of nonrecognized stimuli will perhaps provide some clarification.

Entry to consciousness can be determined from above or below the signal-to-noise ratio, or level of sensory inflow, as well as from factors subject-dependent or stimulus-determined, both of voluntary and of involuntary nature. (Dixon, 1981.) Where visual subliminal messages are concerned, the best known example is the New Jersey theater story. In the 1950s, a New Jersey theater owner reported that he had flashed refreshment subliminals during the showing of the movie *Picnic*. According to claims, flashing the words "Drink Coca-Cola" over Kim Novak's face resulted in a 58 percent increase in Coca-Cola sales over a six-week period.

Literally every sense can be appealed to subliminally, but the stimuli most often used are those that reach either the aural or the visual sense. Generally, videosubliminal stimuli is generated in one of three ways:

1. Slide insertion
2. Candlepower ratio levels
3. Tachistoscope projection

Slide insertion is essentially what was reportedly used in the theater houses in New Jersey. A slide may be inserted as often as one per fourteen frames and usually go consciously unnoticed. A simple visual method for understanding this technique can be produced with a fast-turn card deck of the kind children used to make. By inserting any message once every fourteen to twenty-eight frames and then by thumbing the deck rapidly, you can replicate the type of subliminal exposure involved in the slide insertion process.

The use of candlepower ratio levels involves lowering the light output beneath the wattage of the room lighting. For example, on numerous occasions, I have lectured on subliminal communication using an overhead projector and transparencies for visual support. During most of these presentations, a slide projector with a small wattage bulb presented subliminally (underneath the overhead's brighter light) a three-digit number. The slide of the three-digit number was not consciously visible until the light from the overhead was turned off. This was never done until the audience had responded to a selection test of five alternative three-digit numbers in a multiple choice format. With the light from the overhead projector extinguished, the three-digit slide readily appeared. This simple experiment has regularly produced averages in the correct number selection of over 70 percent. (Chance alone is one in five, or 20 percent.) The slide used no erotic or violent images designed to appeal to the repression mechanism, nor did it employ oedipal or sexual fantasy effects. The slide was never more than this:

Choose #, #, #.

#, #, # is the choice.

In most instances, three integers appeared alone on the slide.

Tachistoscope projection is accomplished by a device that flashes messages every five seconds at a speed of 1/3000th of a second. An average projector with a high-speed shutter can be modified to produce this effect. The tachistoscope itself was patented in 1967 (patent no. 3,060,795) by Precon Process and Equipment Corporation of New Orleans. According to Key in *Subliminal Seduction*, the device was originally used to flash subliminal messages on television and theater screens. Key states that this was the method used by at least one theater during a six-week period to expose 45,699 patrons to the subliminals "Drink Coca-Cola" and "Hungry? Eat Popcorn." Ordinarily, the candlepower method is more effective than the tachistoscope, simply because the message is continuous.

A number of different modalities are involved in audiosubliminal projection as well; however, each method incorporates spoken words beneath a primary carrier. You consciously hear no spoken words, because they are usually concealed in "white" sound, such as wind or water, and/or psychoaccoustically hidden in or beneath music. Nevertheless, if appropriately done and not just substantially lowered in volume, the stimuli is registered.

WHAT YOU PERCEIVE THAT YOU DON'T

You may not hear someone talking to you while you are in a moving automobile with the window down or on a busy street near a construction site; still, the words are sounds that enter the ear on a journey to the brain, where they are converted from electrical impulses to meaningful message units. The words are disguised only from the conscious mind. The conscious mind lacks the ability to discriminate words from sounds, whereas the subconscious mechanically separates verbal messages from noise.

There really is nothing mysterious about subliminal communication, which is natural and can occur throughout the state of being awake or alert. Subliminal communication always has and always will take place, but until the advent of current technology, it was either ignored, unnoticed, or viewed as selective awareness.

With the development of technology, fear and misinformation confused the issue of subliminal communication. Part of the difficulty in understanding subliminal communication rests in the word *subliminal* itself. A subliminal message, at least in the instance of an audiotape, could be defined as a verbal stimulus perceived below the threshold of awareness. Now, the key word here is *perceived*. A whisper two blocks away is below the threshold of awareness, but it is not perceived. Remember that perception in this instance refers to the process of stimuli acknowledged or registered at some level below the threshold of awareness (consciousness). In order for perception by an individual to occur, there must be sufficient stimuli to trigger a neuron in the brain.

For the sake of simplicity, imagine that you are a verbal subliminal stimulus riding beneath the waves of nature sounds and music in the same manner a submarine rides beneath the ocean surface, on a journey into the ear, destined for the brain. The outer ear catches the sound waves as they enter the auditory canal. From the auditory canal the waves are transmitted to the drum membrane, or middle ear, where air pressure and three small bones convey vibrations to the inner ear. Within the inner ear are cochlea, or coiled structures, with sensory cells that receive the sound stimuli and transmit to the brain impulses arising from them. The stimuli ultimately trigger neurons. Millions of neurons are carrying message units triggered by stimuli across the synapses and simultaneously competing for conscious attention.

Neurons have no neutral state. They are either off or on. Therefore, the threshold of awareness, or "perception level," that exists and is taking place below that threshold is in fact a neural excitation. Without neural excitation, there exists no perception. It is noteworthy that research into brain wave activity has confirmed an increase in pattern activity in test subjects who listened to music containing a subliminal message when compared to the subjects listening to the same music without "silent voices." (See chapter 10.)

INFORMATION PROCESSING

Perhaps a model for understanding information processing would be useful here.

Dixon suggests a model that does not require the relationships of consciousness to the brain's capacity to process information. (Dixon, 1981.) I suggest a model that is unlike Dixon's linear models (1981) but that incorporates "wholes" as units of information. Essentially, the information-processing paradigm I suggest is more along the lines of the holographic paradigm of Bohm and Pribram. (See chapter 11.)

Sensory input is neither linear nor directional any more than is information storage in the brain. Sensory input is multidimensional and holographic as is its "parts-to-all" relationship. Just as a piece of a holograph contains a representation of the whole (only diminishing in detail from the whole), a "piece" of information contains explicate other together with an implicate more. Information so totally overwhelms us that only certain important and acceptable stimuli come to conscious awareness. Consciousness in a large sense is the mirror between the object and the holographic plate reflecting directed light (focus and attention) from an object (experience, perception, things) to photographic material (organ brain) upon which the entire (whole) object is dimensionally recorded. In this model the object is the out-there world, the photographic plate is the stuff we call mind (all levels of consciousness individualized, if indeed separable from all consciousness except by selective focus) and the light beam is the life force or animator experiencing itself as individualized consciousness. The light folds around the object in such a manner that part of it is often hidden from itself.

First, a diagram representing a holograph:

21

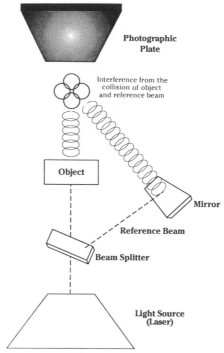

Photographic Plate

Interference from the collision of object and reference beam

Object

Mirror

Reference Beam

Beam Splitter

Light Source (Laser)

Now, here is a holograph as a model of information processing:

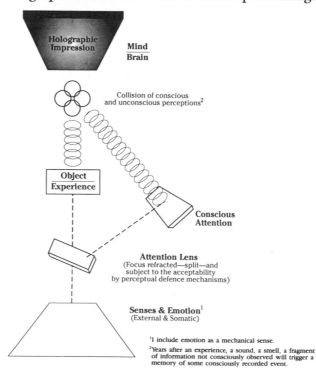

Holographic Impression

Mind / Brain

Collision of conscious and unconscious perceptions[2]

Object / Experience

Conscious Attention

Attention Lens
(Focus refracted—split—and subject to the acceptability by perceptual defence mechanisms)

Senses & Emotion[1]
(External & Somatic)

[1] I include emotion as a mechanical sense.

[2] Years after an experience, a sound, a smell, a fragment of information not consciously observed will trigger a memory of some consciously recorded event.

Impulses, or stimuli, from the senses are relayed to the brain from conscious and nonconscious perceptions. There the total stimuli interfere and converge as they overlap within the cells of the organ (holographic plate) brain. The sum of all interference patterns are distributed and recorded throughout the brain—our own organic hologram.

LIMITED AWARENESS

It has been argued that subjective awareness, or the restriction of awareness content, is a function of consciousness. This restriction gives rise to the possibility for establishing priorities, which are the basis of animal behavior.

There are at least four basic propositions implied in the idea of limited awareness:

1. We process much more information than that of which we are aware.
2. The capacity to process information far exceeds our discernment ability.
3. At some point "unaware information" becomes available to awareness.
4. "Unaware," or subliminal, information can be and is processed unconsciously and may have a profound effect on learning systems and on emotional and physical health.

We know for a fact that anesthetic blocking of the ascending reticular activating system will not prevent evoked responses to external stimuli. Consciousness, or awareness, has been suspended, and yet perception of stimuli occurs.

In my opinion, the definitive objective measurement of subliminal perception is the PET scan (positron emission tomography). At the time of this writing, arrangements are being made to access a PET scan for the purpose of conducting double blind experiments designed to evaluate preferred modalities for providing subliminal stimuli.

SUBLIMINAL SENSORY PERCEPTION

Subliminal stimuli can be perceived at many sensory levels. Subaudible frequencies, such as those associated with silent dog whistles or intense microwave transmissions, and subthreshold electrical shock have been shown to bring about conditioned responses. (See chapter 10.)

The neurophone mechanism has been demonstrated to electronically induce languaged messages through skin contact. The device was originally invented to enable the hearing impaired to enjoy sound, such as Bach fugue. Although allegedly taken off the market by our own National Security Agency, an associate of mine in Canada obtained one for my own inspection and experimentation. An educational psychologist friend and I immediately began experimenting with different levels of communication via the neurophone as compared with similar levels without it. The neurophone has an output control that when raised will cause electronic signals to be "heard" inside the brain as though the sound were generated from outside the ear, and when lowered will pulse the same signal but without sufficient intensity to be consciously perceived.

In every instance in which we employed the neurophone at subthreshold levels, the message was acted upon more consistently than when any type of audible communication, including hypnosis, was employed. The highest correspondence of subaudible messaging to "outside" manifestation by the subject, usually either in dream venting, color meaning tests, or overt behavior, occurred when a subliminal audiocassette was combined with the neurophone and hypnosis. It should be noted, however, that our experimentation was limited to a small sample size and was employed on a client need basis rather than according to a strict scientific design.

The neurophone is best described by its own literature:

> The current hypothesis is based upon the fact that the skin is embryonically the source of all our human sense organs. In fact, the skin itself contains more sensors—for heat, touch, pain, etc.— than any other part of the human anatomy. The human ear evolves embryonically out of the convolutions of the skin of an embryo in the mother's womb. Basically, the skin is the oldest evolutionary nervous system sensor. Since it is the precursor of the ears, it should also be capable of hearing. And, as the Neurophone Mark XI proves, the skin is indeed capable.
>
> Neurologically, the human skin is both piezo-electric and opto-electric. It produces minute electrical currents when vibrated. Soviet

and Czechoslovak neurological research has also shown that the skin produces an electric current when stimulated by light.

As long ago as 1785, Charles Augustin de Coulomb, a French physicist and an early experimenter with electricity, proved that an electrostatic field produces a measurable physical force. The Neurophone Mark XI processes audio information to produce a very weak 20-volt (maximum-RMS) electric field at each of its two transducer disks. This is an alternating electric field that is changed as a function of the *time rate of change* of the audio signal coming into the Neurophone. This minute electric field actually causes microscopic vibrations of the skin under the transducer disks. Maximum coupling of the electric field to the skin is ensured by fabricating the transducer disks from Zirconium Titanate which possesses the same dielectric constant as the human skin.

If you were to put an ordinary medical stethoscope on the skin next to one of the transducer disks during Neurophonic listening, you would be able to detect the minute vibrations of the skin created by the tiny electric field of the transducer disk.

This experiment, conducted initially at Tufts University in 1966, led to the current hypothesis of Neurophonic action.

The working hypothesis of Neurophonic listening is based partially upon work done at Bell Laboratories on the nature of voice communications. It is known that the human voice does not depend upon frequencies. People who have had their larynx removed can use an "artificial larynx," a buzz generator held against the side of the throat. Words—information—are formed totally by the action of the jaw, the tongue, the teeth, the glottis, and the nasal cavities. The human nose and mouth form a highly variable time delay generator. Thus, the basic audio information our brains evolved to decipher, the human voice, is dependent *not* upon frequency (you understand a whisper, a singing tone, or a shouting rasp) but upon the time-rate-of-change nature of sound caused by time delays imposed by the mouth and nasal passages. [Remember this when we later examine time-compressed subliminal stimuli (chapter 7).]

The Neurophone makes use of these research results by processing the incoming audio signal to remove the frequency component and leave only the time domain, the time-rate-of-change information. This is one reason why the Neurophone sounds so scratchy when one first begins to listen to it. The incoming audio signal is doubly differentiated, removing the frequency component. It is then clipped into a square wave type signal. The 20 Volt RMS signal is then sent to the transducer disks. Thus, the electronic circuitry

25

presents audio information to the skin in the way the skin originally evolved to receive and decode the information eons ago.

But is it certain that the Neurophone is not operating by bone conduction as are some other devices available today for listening experiments and enjoyment? A definitive experiment proving that bone conduction is not a cause of neurophonic hearing can be duplicated by anyone with the required simple equipment. It is known as the Batteau Test in honor of the hearing researcher, the late Dr. Dwight Wayne Batteau, who developed the test during Neurophone evaluation at Tufts University.

Two separate channels of audio information are required. One channel goes through a set of ordinary headphones; the other goes through the Neurophone Mark XI. One specific frequency is played through the headphone channel. Another frequency *slightly different* is played through the Neurophone Mark XI circuitry to the transducer disks. If the Neurophone Mark XI were producing hearing by bone conduction, the two slightly different frequencies would "mix" in the bone structures of the inner ear, producing a discernible "beat frequency" which is the difference between the two. With the Neurophone, this "beat frequency" is heard only at very high volume levels in both channels, levels at which the Neurophone probably is producing bone conduction by the strong vibration of the skin under each transducer disk. However, the beat frequency should theoretically be heard at *all* volume levels; it is *not* heard at normal neurophonic listening levels.

The "neurophonic experience" is therefore probably a new way to hear, using the old way discarded by natural evolution eons ago: the skin. (Publisher unknown.)

Hearing via the skin is not limited to the neurophone. Soviet work has effectively demonstrated this for several years. For that matter, seeing via the finger tips, or dermo optics, as it is known, has also been shown to be a trainable phenomenon.

Taking a moment to more completely understand that the sense of hearing is more than sound may help simplify what otherwise might be complex and burdensome. In my attempt to communicate the constructs of subliminal communication through electromagnetic means (sound or light), I will ordinarily refer to the senses of hearing and sight. Still, it is important to understand that either light or sound stimuli can be and are perceived by humans, without use of eyes or ears. Light and sound are simply vibrational frequencies that are converted into or interpreted as electrical signals in the brain. These signals may or may not be of a mechanical nature corresponding to their electromagnetic counterparts (sound and light) in the universe but nevertheless are electrochemical interpretations of electromagnetic stimuli.

HISTORY

The popular history of subliminal communication is really a history of modern subliminal manipulation.

Vance Packard's *Hidden Persuaders*, which appeared in 1957, quoted from the London *Sunday Times* an account of a New Jersey theater in which ice cream ads were flashed onto the screen during a movie showing. That resulted in an otherwise unaccountable increase in ice cream sales. The *Times* referred to this technology as "subthreshold effects."

Packard's work warned of psychologists-turned-merchandisers and of the resulting psychoseduction of the American consumer. From belief systems to product identification, Packard presented a case for persuasion through the art and science of motivational analysis, feedback, and psychological manipulation. *Hidden Persuaders* was the first open attempt to inform the general public of a potentially Orwellian means to enslave the mind and to do so surreptitiously.

Wilson Brian Key in his books *Subliminal Seduction* and *Clam Plate Orgy* argues that not only are we being subliminally merchandised today but the public has been subliminally seduced for hundreds of years. Key, a Canadian professor, sums it all up in the title to his third book on the subject, *The Age of Manipulation*.

In my own work, *Subliminal Communication*, I discussed the earliest modern reference I have found on the subject of subliminal communication. According to Wolman, subliminal research is at least as old as Suslowa's work in 1863 wherein he reported "an increase in the two-point discrimination threshold as a function of subliminal electrical stimulation." (1973.) In 1894, W. R. Dunham, M.D., wrote an interesting commentary on the subliminal mind and subliminal communication. Nearly one hundred years later, Dunham's essay reads much like current research on the subject. In *The Science of Vital Force*, Dunham demonstrated the existence of both subliminal mind and subliminal communication.

A contemporary of Sigmund Freud, Dr. O. Poetzle, studied subliminal perception and the subsequent effect on dreams and behavior days and weeks after the original stimuli. (See chapters 9 and 10.)

One of Freud's most important contributions to approaching the enigma known as the human condition is the stark revelation that mankind is a mere particle of his potential. Unconscious processes predetermine conscious choices and therefore behavior. Aggregates of attitude and behavior constitute personality. Personality is rather rigid, and consequently the human condition is an abysmal shadow of itself. What is more, according to Freud, it is inherently in conflict with itself. Freud, a confirmed atheist, once stated that a belief in God was "a sugar-coated neurotic crutch"; nevertheless, he contributed to the legitimacy of the construct of man's unconscious/subconscious mind.

Professor Wolman modifies Hilgard's categorization of subliminal stimuli, dividing descriptive values into five criteria of awareness and unawareness. The stimulus is—

1. Below the level of registration.

2. Above the level of registration but below the level of detection.

3. Above the level of detection but below the level of stimulus discrimination.

4. Above the level of detection and discrimination but below the level of identification.

5. Below the level of identification only because of a defensive reaction. (1973.)

Wolman makes several general statements regarding subliminal stimulation, having come to certain conclusions based upon his erudite research. Although maintaining a cautious stance, he asserted:

1. Subliminal stimulus does leave an influence upon the content of subsequent cognition.

2. Subliminal stimuli has affected and can affect secondary-process thinking.

3. There are neurophysiological findings which appear to concur with registration without awareness.

4. Despite some failures of replication there are numerous instances where subliminal stimuli "can measurably influence a variety of subject's subsequent behaviors."

28

5. Conscious thinking can be influenced by stimulus outside of awareness. (Ibid.)

In 1981 Dr. Norman Dixon summarized over 748 references on subliminal communication, carefully documenting the effectiveness of subliminal stimulation in his scholarly book *Preconscious Processing*. Dixon provides a model for understanding the flow of information and its entry to consciousness. According to his model, five factors govern whether a stimulus surfaces at a conscious level: direction of attention, signal strength, external noise level, internal noise levels, and signal importance (meaning).

A common misconception regarding subliminal communications is that there are laws protecting the public from their use. That simply is not true. An FCC code prohibits the use of subliminals in electronic communication, but there is no penalty attached to violation of the code. As a result, numerous reports of subliminal messaging in the electronic media exist. As a matter of fact, while I was talking with the show host Martin Davis on a live radio broadcast recently, Mr. Davis informed the radio audience and me of a commercial a major fast-food business had allegedly made using sexual subliminals. He stated that it was then being shown on television. According to Davis, a friend of his associated with this company had shown him the actual footage. The scene presented an attractive woman diving into the water. At the height of the dive a slide of a sea gull was inserted, and just as the woman penetrated the water a slide of a penis was inserted. Sexual embeds in advertising are used to increase dwell time and thus build product awareness. They appeal to the repression mechanism and give rise, it is argued in some instances, to associative pairings of product and mild arousal.

I have personally been involved with legislators who attempted to create laws prohibiting use of subliminal stimuli without informed consent. In Utah this legislation was defeated on the basis of definitional ambiguities. In California the governor vetoed legislation regulating subliminal communication on the basis of unenforceability. Canada enacted statutes governing subliminal communication only to repeal them.

THEORETICAL MODELS OF SUBLIMINAL PERCEPTION

Several theoretical models accommodate subliminal perception within traditional psychology. In fact, it could be asserted that subliminal perception is absolutely implicit within them. Three such models, which are aspects of the psychoanalytic theory of cognition, are set out by Wolman:

> First, there is the "day-residue" model. One kind of day residue is the recent, indifferent, barely noticed, unassimilated impression. According to psychoanalytic theory, such material is "selected" for dreams precisely because of its manifest lack of psychic significance; it resonates with unconscious, infantile wishes and emerges in dreams as a derivative cognitive representation of the drive, owing to the requirements of censorship and the nature of unconscious thinking. The Poetzl experiment and its variants (e.g., Pine 1960) are based on this model, but depart from it in several ways.
>
> The second model is that of Freud's view of preconscious thinking, in which he assumed that such thinking tends to spread out over a wider network of associations than is the case in conscious thought. The direction of preconscious thinking can be biased by unconscious motives and sets ("guiding ideas"). The studies of Spence et al. are based on this model. The subliminal stimulus is expected to bias the preconscious stream of thought, especially if there is a boost from unconscious or conscious motives.
>
> The third model, evident mainly in Silverman's (1967) work, is Freud's conception of unconscious motivation conflict and defense. This model assumes that a subliminal input raises the activation level of existing unconscious motives and that it can therefore be considered analogous to an internally generated increase in the intensity of unconscious motives. (1973.)

Wolman continues:

> These three models are combined in the concept of "schema" activation proposed by Klein and Holt (1960). They assume that memory schemata are activated by sets, by relevant incoming stimuli, and by drives. Under appropriate conditions, marginal inputs are likely to activate drive-related ideas and lead to an effect. This conceptualization is elaborated by Klein (1956, 1970) in terms of a model of motivation in perception which stresses the interplay of executive and concurrently active peripheral motives in relation to their accessibility to awareness, and as determinants of what is focal

versus subsidiary in perceptual experience. If subliminal stimuli are considered as a special case of incidental or peripheral activation, then this model constitutes a promising way to understand the interaction of the variables studied in subliminal research. (Ibid.)

I consider perception to be the fundamental determiner of behavior and favor a modified gestaltian theory of perception; that is, perception is always as *wholes*. Attention is not necessary to perception, and sensations are collective aggregates of information, which by definition of the word *attention* go largely undiscriminated by awareness.

Regardless of perception theories, registration and perception per se are independent, and without an unconscious awareness or subconscious learning dynamic there exists *no* basis to psychology. Drives, motives, and so on, cannot be strictly of conscious perception origin. The unconscious must be more than a repository for the conscious mind's direct (cognitive) experience and/or indirect interpretive accumulation. Be that as it may (or as it may not be, if you prefer), as Wolman states:

"Contrary to popular belief, a good theory is not necessarily one that answers all questions, leaving nothing more to be done in a field, but rather it is one that opens up new problems and new avenues of investigation." (1973.)

THE SUBLIMINAL RESCRIPTING MODALITY

It is my opinion that subliminal communication is used to exploit, and yet it can be used for beneficial purposes, too. It *is* the most powerful modality for self-improvement currently available. It can literally rescript the preconscious mind, stripping away negative expectations and self-doubt and replacing these destructive patterns with positive input, thereby bringing about desired behavior changes in an effortless and natural way—from the inside out.

The unconscious mind contains within it our biocomputer programming. Most of us have acquired this programming in much the same way as we acquired our basic language. Without our conscious choice, subliminal beliefs have been scripted. Repeated experiments have adequately demonstrated that the conscious

31

mechanism is not a necessary part of information processing. In fact, the unconscious can and quite frequently does operate without, or at least unknown to, the conscious mechanism. This preconscious discernment has long been studied. (See chapter 10.)

Where preconscious predisposition is concerned, Benjamin Libet of the University of California believes that conscious intention only facilitates or inhibits action initiated by the preconscious process. In fact, according to the *Brain/Mind Bulletin*'s report on Libet's work, correlations between EEG patterns and conscious experience reveal that 350 milliseconds before the subjective experience of, say, wanting to move, distinct activity in brain-wave patterns occurs. Libet views this model as understanding choice. We choose to act or not to act, but we do not necessarily choose what to act upon.

The human biocomputer, the subconscious mind, is the most sophisticated neuroautomechanism ever imagined. Its capabilities are absolutely mind-boggling. Nevertheless, most of us have never programmed this wonderful human attribute with programs of our choosing. Computer programmers have a term that applies to what most of us have unwittingly done: GIGO, meaning "garbage in, garbage out." For years I have spoken of what I term a socioenculturated *no-don't* syndrome without *yes-do* rights of passage. The result all too often is self-doubt, fear, rejection, and other paralyzing expectations. These expectations are so powerful that for some they become addictions—and as with any addiction, each addictive experience portends another of the same kind.

In a very simple sense, subliminals are an antidote for the self-poisoning of the subconscious script. What they can do can be referred to by a different nonsense term, one I call PIPO, meaning "positive in, positive out." Their immediate efficacy is due to the fact that the conscious mind cannot argue with their positive content and thereby diminish them. Subliminals go directly into the subconscious and immediately begin to reprogram the old biocomputer scripts, replacing doubt, fear, and negative attitudes and expectations in general with powerful new positive computations.

There is no law of limitation except that which is self-imposed. Research supporting this fact shows us that personal limitations are almost always the result of negative programming that has created beliefs and expectations in the subconscious mind. The subconscious mind, acting as the biocomputer, actually governs much of our conscious behavior, emotions, addictions, and attitudes. Thus, subliminal communication offers an affordable alternative to the self-help consumer and a powerful ancillary tool to the health care professional.

CHAPTER FOUR

DEFINITIONS AND TECHNOLOGY

What man cannot collectively intuit and understand, he defines. My postman friend Al once defined a kiss as an anatomical juxtaposition of two orbicularis oris muscles in a state of contraction. Isn't it wonderful that things are not their definitions?
                            —*Eldon Taylor*

WORKING TOWARD A DEFINITION

One of the difficulties with both legislative attempts and communication in general concerning subliminals, for expert and layperson alike, is the broad scope of the definition of subliminal stimuli.

Subliminal technically means any form of communication not consciously perceived. Therefore the use of such phraseology as *subliminal perception*, for example, is awkward, because the terms are mutually exclusive unless the meaning of *perception* is stretched to include any level of perception—conscious or unconscious. Research clearly shows that information is somehow processed from stimuli received but not consciously apprehended. It is in this sense that stretching the literal meaning of the word *perception* is intended. Data assembled by psychologists, neurobiologists, and neurologists strongly support the notion that all sensory input is from at least two levels of perception—conscious and unconscious. And more than one notable thinker is of the opinion that no significant belief originates on the basis of data consciously perceived.

For purposes here, the following stratification of word usage and meaning apply:

Supraliminal means perceivable, albeit not always recognized as such. Associations, such as a politician and a baby, and contextual inferences are examples of visual/auditory presentations that normally are consciously unnoticed.

Subception refers to something ordinarily not perceivable by the conscious mind because of the operation of one or more defense mechanisms. An example would be a taboo embed, such as that used by *Playboy's* subscription ad and the wreath of genitalia (discussed in detail in my *Subliminal Communication: Emperor's Clothes or Panacea?).*

Subliminal is that which cannot be assessed by the conscious mind because of some technical application that masks accessibility and that cannot be made accessible except by electronic unmasking techniques.

Now, with these definitions in place, *supraliminal communication* covers ordinary communication that may have unconscious communication inherent in it, and *subception* refers to manipulation of the kind sometimes used by advertisers in print media. Both of these forms of communication are accessible to the trained observer without the technical assistance of special equipment or instrumentation.

On the other hand, *subliminal communication* refers to communication created by technical assistance (equipment, instruments, technology in general) that simply cannot be perceived directly by the conscious mind, irrespective of the training or sophistication about such matters on the part of the observer. For example, if a sound engineer back-masks a spoken message in a heavy-metal recording (subliminal stimuli), the listener does not possess the conscious ability to perceive the subliminal in the finished product without technical assistance from special instrumentation.

Wherever *subliminal* appears in this text, the word means stimuli or process not consciously perceived (e.g., subliminal messages are stimuli, whereas subliminal mind refers to process dynamics). Terms such as *preconscious processing*, *subliminal mind*, and so on refer to the information (stimuli) process dynamics. *Mind* is treated as conscious, subconscious, unconscious, and so forth, as distinguished from location: brain. *Process* refers to mind whereas *mechanics* refers to operational functions of the brain. *Silent voices* is just my own break from the repetition of the word *subliminal* and is intended as a synonym for verbal subliminal stimuli.

PERCEPTUAL DEFENSE MECHANISMS

Perceptual defense mechanisms play a significant role in why we sometimes fail to recognize consciously what we see. In a real sense, what we expect to see is what we do see. Carrol's metaphor of rose-colored glasses is a descriptively accurate parable for much of our perception. Consequently, it might be valuable to review the basic perceptual defense mechanisms.

Denial. As implied by its name, this mechanism is simply one of denying. Often the denial occurs through projection, that is, projecting blame or fault on another.

Fantasy formation. This mechanism creates a perceived reality out of fantasy. If motives cannot be satisfied in the objective external world, they may become a reality in an internal dream world. Some psychologists suggest that the appeal for much of our entertainment is satisfaction oriented to our fantasies for adventure, affection, and security, perhaps not so vividly experienced otherwise.

Introjection. Introjection places blame on oneself. This self-directed blame or punishment defends against disappointment or disillusionment from another. For example, a child feels unworthy of a parent's attention because the parent pays no attention to the child.

Isolation. This mechanism involves the avoidance of connecting associations to related ideas that produce anxiety. One set of data is isolated from an associated set: birth is isolated from death, war from mourning, nuclear arsenals from murderous horror.

Projection. Simply stated, this mechanism allows one to project blame, fantasy, and so on upon another.

Regression. This mechanism is common during serious illness. Essentially, it means that one regresses to an earlier age, usually to a stage of development where someone else assumed responsibility and where fewer, simpler, and more primitive goals existed.

Repression. Generally this mechanism censors or prohibits memories, associations, and adjustments from conscious awareness. Like an invisible filter, this mechanism prevents the conscious mind from "seeing" painful memories or "stymied" motives. Personal experiences ranging from embarrassment to cruelty are often subject to the lens of repression.

Sublimation. This mechanism is the redirection of basic drives. Sublimation is simply the substitution of acceptable behavior to satisfy basic motives that might be met equally well in a primitive sense by some form of social behavior. For example, basic aggression motives are often met by sports activities. The process of sublimation is to find avenues in which basic motives may be satisfied in a manner acceptable to the individual and to society.

In addition, there are miscellaneous escapes and defenses that some theorists consider as contributing to the basic perceptual defenses mentioned above, all for the purpose of showing each of us only what we want to see about ourselves and about the world around us.

It should be noted also that many mechanisms can be functioning at one time; in those instances, the boundaries overlap, making it difficult to differentiate between the mechanisms.

THE AFFECTIVE INFLUENCE

Eight areas of human activity have been identified as being demonstrably affected by subliminal communication:

37

1. Conscious perception
2. Dreams
3. Drives
4. Emotions
5. Memory
6. Perceptual defenses
7. Value norm anchor points
8. Verbal behavior

Conscious perception presupposes that the way we see the world is within a system of "sets." Most behavioral scientists credit the enculturation process with this predisposition. The sets are often referred to by political scientists as ethnocentric. Means for coping with and evaluating good and bad, right and wrong within a society are constructed through the use of sets. For example, facial expressions and body language in general are often paired with the use of language to give rise to different meanings. According to Key, in his work *Subliminal Seduction*, interpretation of facial expressions has been demonstrated to be influenceable by subliminal stimuli. In other words, a basically expressionless face can be seen as an angry expression if the viewer is exposed simultaneously to the word *anger* at a subliminal level. (1974.)

Dreams constitute one of our clearest empirical accesses to unconscious processes. Dreams often process subliminally perceived stimuli. Key cites several instances of individuals dreaming "out" subliminally perceived stimuli from researchers' work with particular taboo embeds found in commercial advertising. Key also suggests that subliminal perception is close kin to posthypnotic suggestion. Since posthypnotic suggestions can be and often are erased from conscious awareness by another suggestion for partial amnesia, Key suggests that the functional aspect of both are more alike than not. (Ibid.)

Dreams very often are passages to otherwise hidden, unresolved conflict. It is not at all uncommon for a therapist to have a dream reported that brings this conflict to the surface after a session utilizing a dichotic or amnesive approach as an uncovering technique; but that can also be said for any other normally acceptable therapeutic intervention or uncovering modality.

Emotions are among the most responsive of all human behavioral characteristics to be affected by subliminal communication. The ability of subliminal input to excite, arouse, anger, or desensitize us to external stimuli is well established in the literature and will be discussed in more detail later in this chapter as well as in chapters 10 and 11.

Memory has been increased by the aid of subliminal perception. It should also be noted that memory is a complex process. Ordinarily discussion is about conscious memory, but unconscious memory also exists.

Because our defense mechanisms function the way they do, many memories become undesirable and are stored away in the unconscious. It can be further said that many one-time useful memories have also slipped out of conscious memory into the subconscious/unconscious. And there is unconscious processing going on that the conscious never was aware of. These are unconscious memories.

Additionally, there is associative memory, that is, memory of something consciously perceived because of stimuli simultaneously unconsciously perceived and yet connectively associated. One good, although in my opinion irresponsible, example of this type of memory can be illustrated by the work of educational psychologist Dr. Bruce R. Ledford. Ledford theorized that if advertisers could increase product identification subliminally, learning could be enhanced in a similar manner. He proceeded to expose students at East Texas State University to erotic and violent pictures projected subliminally on a screen behind him as he lectured. The slides were shown at one candlepower above the light in the classroom and were therefore consciously imperceptible. Ledford's lectures, which had nothing to do with the slides being projected, were apparently more interesting to the students than in the past, as indicated by test scores. Test results indicated a significant increase in memory relevant to the material presented by Ledford, as compared to students of a control group who viewed only a blank screen behind Ledford's lectures. (Taylor, 1986; see chapters 10 and 11.)

Perceptual defenses protect us from shocking or deeply traumatic material. Our perceptual defenses can actually assist a subliminal manipulation by shutting out data we might otherwise perceive. Tantamount to this is Key's example of the Howard Johnson menu in his *Clam Plate Orgy*. An orgy scene is not what we expect to find in an illustration of a plate of clams on a menu in a prom-

39

inent and respected restaurant. Simply speaking, we refuse to see what is there to be seen. (1981.)

Value norm anchor points are positions selected by an individual as a reference point between opposites. It is from these points that we evaluate ourselves and the world around us. It is a personally/culturally acceptable position between good and bad, right and wrong, success and failure, approval and rejection, and so forth. Numerous studies report that subliminally perceived data can move these anchor points.

Verbal behavior is a complex construct. As it relates to our interest within the scope of subliminal use, there are at least three aspects to be considered:

1. Multiple meaning permutations
2. Explicit/implicit set
3. Contextual reference

Multiple meaning permutations refer to words that contain other words with drastically different meanings. (Consider the *con* in confidence.) This category also refers to implications or associations, such as the vegetable *pea* and the action *pee*. Key, in *Subliminal Seduction*, states that certain taboo four-letter words are also implied in seemingly innocuous verbiage. Key selected such words as *whose* (*whore*) and *cult* (*cunt*) to demonstrate strong emotional responses at a subliminal level. Key claims that words of this nature are deliberately used in ad copy to build emotional content. Key also refers to a broad scope of experiments that demonstrate that these emotion-laden words evoke physiological responses that can be measured on an electroencephalograph. (1974.)

Explicit/implicit and contextual reference in verbal response and behavior are necessarily interconnected. Where explicit and implicit are concerned, the manner in which our primary caretaker communicated with us provides a model for whether we interpret language literally (explicit) or by inference (implicit), or both.

If, for example, our primary caretaker (usually mother) gave us instructions that were inconsistent, we became inferential. For the sake of clarity, let us say mom sent you to your room with instructions not to come out until it was clean. Let's say you did come out of your room without first cleaning it, and she was in the kitchen preparing dinner. Now, assume you asked mother what was for dinner, and she responded by telling you to get out of the kitchen, to go outside and play. You begin to interpret mother inferentially by what she *really* means. As a result, you become an implicit, or inferential, learner. (See chapter 5.)

If, however, mother was literal and direct, with few inconsistencies, you become a literal, or explicit, learner. The conceptual nature of your verbal behavior or behavior connected with language meaning is derived from the context of learning and usage. A simple example of that is the profanity used by a comic versus the same profanity expressed in a hostile manner.

Additionally, language is full of intoned qualities, psychophysical response mechanisms, and denotative and connotative imbuements. Consequently, the meaningful power of negative scripting is much more than just the words used.

Other areas of human activity that subliminal communication can and does affect are suggested by clinical data. One of major interest to me is the connection between mind and body and the apparent power the mind has to instruct the cells. Given this capacity, cancers have been controlled, breasts have been enlarged, sight has been restored, and much more. Perhaps the study of subliminal communication will turn out to be in part the study of psychophysical interrelatedness. One thing is certain, whether it is biocomputer programming through images and words or the power of expectation from a sugar pill, the body chemistry is affected and heals itself. I have been amazed that science has for so long developed pharmacology and discounted the placebo effect. It occurs to me that developing placebos would have unraveled much more of the mind-body connection and by now perhaps provided insight into the mind's ability to heal or to slay. It is my opinion that the time will come when most disease of the body will be understood as dysfunction of the mind. Somehow a mix-up in messaging occurs, perhaps due to our need to punish ourselves, obtain attention, take a break from the ordinary routine, or escape some pressure situation. The real mix-up is between the conscious and the subconscious, not the brain and the body. And indeed, I believe health care professionals will be more diagnostic oriented than cure oriented in the future. The responsibility for the dysfunction will fall squarely on the shoulders of self-cure via self-discovery.

41

THE TECHNOLOGY

With these definitions in place, we can now review the technology. Videosubliminal stimulation methods were sufficiently discussed in chapter 3, but audiosubliminal stimulation methods were not. The nuances of audiosubliminal presentations are widely varied. Some companies "time-compress" their verbal messaging by either speeding up the human voice to high pitched squeals or by digitally compressing it, which is the process of removing the spacing between sounds, thus delivering one continuous noise. Other companies multifrequency statements, often in ranges that an ordinary cassette player cannot reproduce and which audiologists inform us are imperceptible. All of this seems to be designed to sell a "more is better" mentality to the public. Claims for hundreds of thousands of messages on a sixty-minute audiocassette seem ridiculous to me. Language is a learned skill; it is *not* mechanical, like the response to color or to dream imagery. Negative languaging that exists in the biocomputer exists there and has power because of the meaningfulness with which it was delivered. It is my opinion that we would be better served with a program in a foreign language said meaningfully than with sounds the conscious mind is unable to translate even if they were fully audible.

Opinions aside, since the literature and the evidence for subliminal communication to be presented, with one exception, is based upon meaningfully created statements said slowly and with purpose, a discussion of the exotic claims and methods will be limited for the moment to those just discussed.

Still, there exist a number of popular and proven methods for delivering verbal subliminal stimuli. The first is one of concealing straightforward statements. The second is known as back-masking, or metacontrast. The third uses both simultaneously. My own research, to be discussed later in the text, suggests a preference for using both, but by tasking the hemispheres differently in terms of verbal content. This approach is called hemispheric brain synchronization, or the "whole brain" approach. (See chapter 7.)

It is well known that in a very real sense every human being has two brains. These two brain hemispheres are commonly referred to as the right and the left brain. For the vast majority of people, the left hemisphere is the analytical brain and the right hemisphere

42

is the spatial brain. The left hemisphere is in charge of such things as mathematical and language skills, whereas the right hemisphere is the creative and emotional center. The right hemisphere is indiscriminate; the left logical and rational, with defense mechanisms built around logic and reason. Most researchers relegate logic and conscious reasoning to the left hemisphere and emotional and subconscious learning to the right hemisphere.

Hemispheric technology appeals to the two hemispheres appropriately according to the primary hemispheric function. The left brain is interested in literal correctness, whereas the right is more interested in overall associations or relationships. It is believed that the left brain views language literally and according to the *rules* of language, whereas the right brain views language spatially and emotionally, tumbling the words in a process called subconscious cerebration, and even seeing the words as our eyes see the world—upside down.

Some heavy metal music recordings have included subliminal messages (almost always satanic, drug, or sexual in orientation) for years. These messages seem to appeal directly to emotions, causing behavior to override reason. They are also recorded in reverse, a process known as metacontrast or back-masking. Reversing, or playing backwards, subliminal messages in heavy metal music appears to excite emotional expressions and responses often viewed as right brain in their origin.

In the whole-brain approach, on one channel, accessing the left brain, are meaningfully spoken, forward-masked, permissive affirmations delivered in a round-robin manner by a male voice, a female voice, and a child's voice. Research shows that individuals may respond more favorably according to their preference of male, female, or child voices. On another channel, accessing the right brain, directive messages, in the same voices, are recorded in metacontrast. Since the hemispheres are task oriented, both the left and right brain become involved according to their specialties.

Continuing with the learnings from our research and where our own technology is concerned, we include a couple of other nuances. The voices are recorded in round robin fashion with echo and reverberation. (We will describe this construct further when we discuss split-brain studies in chapter 9.) The tracks are mixed through a special processor an electronics engineer and I designed to convert sound frequencies to electrical impulses and track the subliminal message, synchronizing it in stereo with the primary carrier as shown below:

The mixer, known as the PAR processor (PAR: Progressive Awareness Research), maintains minimum volume differences and, with the round-robin echo-reverb, ensures that none of a message is lost. The only other certain way to do this is to have continuous music without breaks or great differences in movements, or to combine white or pink sound, such as ocean surf, with the music. The duration of breaks in the music (primary carrier) is still of utmost concern.

The first of the subliminal tracking mixers was developed by Professor Hal Becker of Tulane University. Known as the "black box," Becker's device was used to mix spoken words with Muzak. Becker's process was tested in a supermarket in New Orleans during 1979. The black box mixed "Thou shalt not steal" and "Honesty is the best policy" into the Muzak system broadcast in the store. Reported lowering of cash shortages, inventory damage, and pilferage was astounding.

Becker's resourcefulness as both researcher and entrepreneur led to the creation of weight-loss programs that worked. Not only did the participants lose weight but their losses were not regained. In 11 percent of the instances, the maintained weight loss was 25 percent; for 50 percent more, the maintained loss was 50 percent; and for the remaining 24 percent, the maintained loss was between 75 to 100 percent over a two-year period.

Becker's process was also used at McDonagh Medical Center to eliminate patient fainting and for the most part was able to establish the credibility of audiosubliminals.

The Becker black box is used today by a commercial company, Mind Communications, to produce audiosubliminals for consumers. Dr. Paul Tuthill, founder of Mind Communications, has been a leader in providing candid consumer information about subliminal communication.

Another manufacturer of subliminal properties to develop a mixing system similar to that of Mind Communications is the Institute of Human Development, also known as Gateways.

Electronic processing in the mixing of subliminal properties ensures a constant signal differential betweeen primary carrier (music) and subliminal content (verbal message) that is critical to the registration process and obviously, therefore, to the replication of scientific findings.

CHAPTER FIVE

How We Learn

*The highest order of our achievement
is probably served more by inhibition
than excitation.—Carl Lauprecht*

Learning

When it comes to understanding complex synergisms, models are very helpful. Looking at how we learn and how we act out that learning is one such complex interaction of elements occurring simultaneously and resulting in a synergistic totality known as the individual.

In research, behavioral scientists provide data and theories that support the *average* aggregate of observations, then apply this to the individual. Yet we know that no two individuals are alike and no one individual is the average. Just as theories make general assumptions about the individual that are not necessarily representative of any one individual, so do models generalize in making a statement about reality when in fact the model is self-defining and does not necessarily say anything about reality. A dear friend of mine, Professor William Guillory (former chairman of the Chemistry Department at the University of Utah) states that even models of "hard science" are self-defining and may say nothing valid about reality. This is not to say that models are not useful or to suggest that remedies may not be derived specific to an individual or a population, for quite obviously such a statement would be absurd!

Nevertheless, with this introduction in mind, let us examine whether a couple of models of the mind can be helpful in understanding why subliminal technology is so effective. Before examining the first model I wish to make clear one of my biases. Most behavioralists assert that there are three ways in which we learn:

1. Trial and error
2. Rote core
3. Condition-response

I believe that all learning is essentially condition-response. Trial and error employs the obvious feedback systems of both the physical and the psychological aspects of a person. For example, with learning as basic as that involved in walking, both the pain from falling and the emotional encouragement given during the learning process form response conditioning. Concerning rote core memory, the stimuli intensity is directly proportional to the memory retention. The stronger the stimulus (incentive), the more favorable the learning—at least to the point of overstimulation. After that the learning is dramatically inhibited. Stimulus-response is condition-response learning.

Dr. John Kappas has created a model of learning and behavior in which he suggests that we assimilate learning either through literal and direct means or through inference, and that the vast majority of us do so primarily in one fashion or the other—not both simultaneously. (We discussed this briefly in chapter 4.) For most of us, our primary caretaker (ordinarily our mother) is responsible for our "suggestibility," the way we learn (literal or inferential), and our secondary caretaker (usually father) creates our "sexuality," the way we act out our learning (emotionally or physically). In a very real sense this forms the basis for acceptance, rejection, and interpretation of the various message units we receive in a lifetime. (Kappas, 1978.)

Since our brains are tasked hemispherically, the synthesis of our suggestibility and sexuality often produces hemispheric dominance. Thus, we may assert something that immediately is consciously rejected or repressed. Whenever the logic center comes into conflict with the emotional center, the emotionally conditioned response will always prevail.

Now, with this model in mind, let us examine a simplified biocomputer analogy and superimpose it upon our model. Every message unit that we receive in a lifetime is imprinted upon our preconscious mind. This process occurs largely without discrimination, except for the lenses of interpretation, which themselves are a direct result of our primary and secondary caretakers and of the enculturation process in general. This imprinting provides the basis of moral value judgments and notions of reality, together with a general attitude regarding change or the incorporation of new ideas.

Statistically, we all receive many more negative than positive message units during maturation. Our society has no "rites of passage" in which we can leave behind all of what I referred to earlier as the "no-don't garbage." Consequently, as adults our garbage often becomes our anchors, and thus our ability to navigate the seas of life are limited to our own safe and sometimes shallow waters. For most of us, then, "safe" waters provide boundaries or self-imposed limitations. These safe waters inhibit much new experience. As an example, unless we are born to success and prosperity, we do not expect to succeed and prosper because the waters surrounding our anchor do not include any such bounty.

This programming means we are behaviorally predisposed by the preconscious, which manifests as lack of confidence, fear of failure, internalization of stress, physical ailments, and rationalization. Most, if not all, of this conditioning takes place in primitive ways so far as the function of learning and behavior is concerned. The old fight/flight mechanisms used by our ancestors give rise to deeply impressed self-limiting behavior. Let us attempt to examine this graphically.

In the drawing below, the circle represents the total mental process, and in the deepest levels of consciousness exist the fight/flight (knee-jerk) mechanisms. All of our input is represented by the pluses and minuses of experience (condition-response) learning. As you can see, the fight/flight response has been replaced in our modern society by anxiety and depression. (Ibid.) The double arrow system illustrates stimuli from the outside world—both real and synthetic. To illustrate, a real stimulus might be a tiger in hot pursuit while a synthetic stimulus is one in which no real danger exists. The mind, however, responds to both real and synthetic stimuli according to the interpreted emotional intensity of the stimuli.

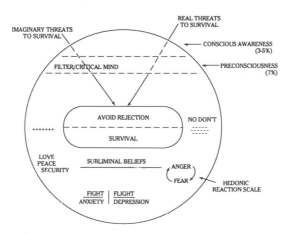

I suggest that few of us have been presented with much real stimuli, that all of the stimuli that condition self-limiting responses are synthetic. I suggest further that this stimuli is based upon an innate fear of isolation and that rejection by another human being or the fear of rejection conditions nearly all of our responses.

Our initiative and response is built upon our perception of "others" and our need for acceptance and understanding. Thus, behavior is purely condition-response learning! In most instances choice is only an illusion, because only limited choices exist and those choices result from the patterns of our conditioning.

Fear of rejection inhibits who and what we are or become. Spending a lifetime projecting ourselves for acceptance is self-alienation in its normal condition. Robert Laing, in *Politics of Experience*, says mankind has educated itself to become absurd and thus to become normal.

Genius has been defined as the quality of seeing the same things others see but seeing them differently. But genius requires giving up everything to gain perhaps nothing. Einstein had to give up Newtonian physics together with all of his vested interests attached thereto in order to discover that space was curved and relatively ruled.

On many occasions Professor William Guillory and I have lectured on the risk factor involved in creativity and its subliminal workshop interface. A subliminal program (audiocassette) essentially carries on a workshop with the subliminal mind. One day the subliminal mind (subconscious, preconscious, unconscious) challenges the conscious (a highly integrated reflection of a much larger form of consciousness) with new ideas, realizations, and uncoverings. When this challenge occurs, risk is discovered. In order to become something (or someone) else—say, self-empowered—we must give up what we are. The self-empowered are truly the self-responsible. Thus, one day we realize that no one else, no other thing, no outside stimulus is to blame for who and what we are. We made all the choices. We elected to deal or cope with external stimuli by adapting our behavior. Our behavior is only an outer manifestation of our inner beliefs. Our beliefs are always based upon our experience. Our experience is limited by our need for acceptance. Acceptance, more often than not, requires surrendering ourselves to become that which others desire. Our social fabric enculturates socially accepted players. Each player chooses the form of adaptive behavior that provides the least amount of risk, and the cycle is self-perpetuating.

Working with incarcerated people, I have heard many reasons (rationalizations, projections) for the social alienation that led to the imprisonment of inmates. "My mother was a prostitute," "my daddy was an alcoholic," "the neighbor boy hung heroine on me when I was a kid" are some of the more exaggerated claims that displace responsibility for criminally irresponsible behavior.

We all have a basic drive to find acceptance and a primitive mechanism to preserve the species from self-destruction. Understanding these facts is fundamental to deciphering the "victim" role of the criminal. In this model, the criminal preserves his self-image by becoming the victim. After all, basically he is a good person (true self-hate will produce suicide or other self-destructive actions, which are not the province of this issue or this book) who acted against society and self in a justified manner and with the least amount of risk. It might have been easier to go along with "them" (peers) than to resist, or, in totally criminal life-styles, the chosen behavior is defined by the participant as more rewarding than its alternative and/or as addictive by codependent learnings.

DIFFERENCES AND SIMILARITIES

M. Scott Peck, in his book *People of the Lie*, provides a model wherein the best of us become criminals by definition, going undetected. Outwardly people of the lie display appropriate and even praiseworthy behavior, but privately they brutalize themselves, their acquaintances, and their loved ones. They do so with hate, anger, revenge, ridicule, and all of those limiting behaviors that oppose unconditional love, all the while believing such conduct is normal and necessary to the human condition. Each thought and act away from love and acceptance is destructive to human potential. Every act of anger is an act away from the inclusive domain of self-responsibility. We lack the ability to self-empower to the precise degree we act against ourselves by betraying this principle.

The one who may feel uncomfortable or resist this proposition is the one who is always unwilling to forgive someone or something. Forgiveness is what risking is all about. Forgiving self and all others provides the opportunity to view the world differently. The old system has never worked. Kind has begotten kind since time began. Hate, anger, greed, and lust are not necessary to the human condition. No productive value is served by shackling ourselves with limitations.

There are at least two ways to be tied up. One is for someone else to bind you; another is for you to hold onto something. Like a string tethered to a door knob, so long as you hold onto it, you cannot leave the perimeter of its length. Beliefs can be like so many strings that prevent movement. And the irony of it all is that when you see the belief from the perspective of its origin, it becomes difficult to hold onto despite the usual efforts.

Thus:

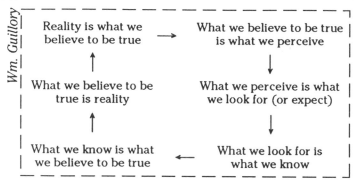

In order to escape the circularity of this, we must give up what we are afraid to give up first—or at least suspend the belief or hold it in abeyance. Albert Einstein once stated that imagination was more important than knowledge. Learning is dynamic activity, and creativity is the highest order of learning. Moreover, creativity is among the highest acts of consciousness. Letting go of finite aspects of knowledge provides the opportunity to learn in the highest order. Synthesizing aspect learning in a dynamic way builds awareness levels which ultimately can culminate in one mind (knowing all levels of self-consciousness) engaging in the continual process of learning.

A Sufi master once said that knowing the difference between the container and the contents would reveal all. Thought is play preparing and selecting perception and experience. In *Science, Order, and Creativity*, David Bohm asserts:

> Another way of defending the subliminal structure of ideas is to overemphasize the separation between a particular problem and other areas: In this way the problem can be studied in a limited context and without the need to question related concepts. . . . . .
>
> Clearly the problems with thought is that it often fails to be perceptively sensitive to similarities and differences and instead applies mechanical habits of seeing similarities and differences. (Bohm and Peat, 1987.)

Understanding, at least in some overall conceptual way, the manner in which we learn and the basic drives behind the learning choices and mechanisms will become very important when we review some of the findings about subliminal communication and then look at the future of subliminal communication. We can then be "perceptively sensitive" to differences and similarities, recognizing that differences often teach similarities.

REVIEW

In review, then, and once again with simple models for the purpose of reaching some point of common perspective necessary to communication:

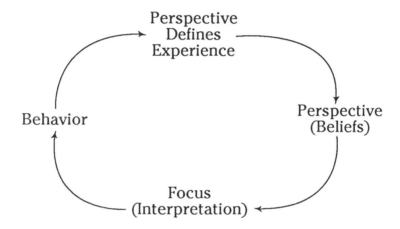

A shift in perspective will produce a general shift in experience. The shift from the "normal" way of being to the more "natural" way of being sets aside for the moment the perceived need to be "normal" and therefore accepted. The creative result occurs because the artifacts of aspect knowledge, no matter how long and hard we have worked to acquire them, are viewed as nothing so important as to prevent us from risking into the process of learning.

One certainty about science is that it will change. Each level of learning will give way to still another unfolding meaning, which will teach similarity from difference, wholeness from parts, synergisms from individuation, and outerness from innerness. As Aeschylus said:

> Nothingness is the only meaningful aspect of the universe. For it allows total unrestrained creativity. True openness is creativity. It

53

is allowing one's self to be channeled with the creative spark, and the manifestation is a function of the talents and preparation of the physical entity; no matter what form. The secrets of the universe are not secret—they are ever unfolding. (Quoted in Guillory, 1988.)

CHAPTER SIX

THE REJECTION LOOP

Ignorance precedes knowing.
To know is to love.
In ignorance there is less than love,
yet ignorance teaches love.
To the precise degree
we are ignorant,
we are that much less
than we could become.
What we could become is
who we really are.
—Eldon Taylor

LIMITED MAN

What many modern psychologists fail to take into account when reviewing and adopting the models of learning and behavior is their often atheistic Freudian view. As such, psychophysical properties are all that Freud's lens was capable of interpreting; and all that was interpreted was modeled according to the perception that limited man was all man could ever be. Freud, while contributing substantially to the acceptance of a mind level usually not consciously accessible, reduced man to pure animal complicated by reason and intelligence. In *The Future of an Illusion*, Freud asserts that for man to aspire to any other condition for himself or to experience the self-actualization principle of Maslow is ludicrous and neurotic. In Freud's words:

> We shall tell ourselves that it would be very nice if there were a God who created the world and was a benevolent Providence, and if there were a moral order in the universe and an after-life; but it is a very striking fact that all this is exactly as we are bound to wish it to be. (1961.)

For Freud, anything other than "wretched" man was a creation of man's needs to make tolerable his helplessness—especially the helpless memories of childhood. Freud's own limitedness was mitigated only by his awareness of this basic human propensity.

Now, the purpose here is not the issue of God, but rather the contextual nature of Freud's own bias and its predetermined prejudice upon the models developed therefrom to define much of the human condition. For Freud, differences were indeed stark. Man has many illusions which are inherent to his drives and motives; one such illusion is the notion that man is more than a collection of organs in an artifact world; that notion, according to Freud, is nothing more than a cherry-flavored neurotic panacea.

Freud's model of behavior arises out of blame and must therefore be built with blame as a natural and inescapable process man participates in, a process that further generates itself in man. Blame displaces responsibility, and therefore man is only responsible insofar as he responds appropriately to his miserable predicament. Appropriate response is of course the socially acceptable, and adaptive behavior is the normative function of coping. Coping is a constant trade-off between the self's wants and desires, imagination and fantasy, love and hate on one side and acceptance by socially appropriate standards on the other. According to this paradigm, man is necessarily in conflict with himself and his societal needs. Man's values are intrinsic to precedence, as secular humanists might argue. That is, he chooses his values as part of his primitive survival instincts. To choose not to honor another's rights provides precedent for pure survival of the fittest behavior. Thus, like it or not, man struggles with the difference between primitive drives and needs and socially acceptable behavior. Many of man's so-called defense mechanisms can exist only by assuming these component principles as implicit to man.

This entire process is termed sublimation. But more than being just one of the defense mechanisms, sublimation must exist in order for the remaining mechanisms to have more than just construct value. Sublimation is indeed the situation, according to this model, as well as a particular defense mechanism.

MAN AS VICTIM

All of this model presupposes man as a victim in the universe—a nonpermanent entity struggling to become what he is and cannot be—fighting back primitive instincts, suppressing and building in a flux scenario such constructs as ego. And in the opinion of many, all of that is nonsense—pure, unmitigated, rubbish. Just as with Newtonian physics, it is helpful and functional as far as it goes, but it is not sufficient to deal with the whole of the human condition.

Man is a victim only of his fears. The teleology of man's motives, in their innate order, or hierarchy of purpose, is:

First: Self-interest. Our level-one responses are wired into the spinal system. Every single cell of our being is designed to preserve itself.

Second: Species interest. The four basic drives of man have been defined in most instances as fight, flight, food, and the propagation of the species. Level-two responses are hypothalamic, ranging from body temperature to propagation.

Third: Highest intellect. When something in nature really matters, it exists in nature in abundance. As Professor Carl Lauprecht from the University of California at San Francisco has pointed out, nature has provided man with abundant cortex. The cortex is man's cognitive inhibitor. (1987.) Level-three "stuff" is essentially conceptual, or cognitive. The inhibitory process begins in the cortex. The cortex stops or reverses signals from the reticular activating system (RAS).

The RAS has both psychophysiological and physiological functions. The RAS turns on the diencephalon (thalamus and hypothalamus) as well as the cortical area. When there is low reticular arousal, there is low behavioral response, and, conversely, an electroencephalograph (EEG) is a quantification of input from RAS to cortex. The RAS is the primary excitation source (gas pedal) of the human energy system. It is connected to nearly all parts of the brain. The thalamus sorts the messages the RAS sends the cortex. In a sense, the RAS is like an early-warning system—it turns the whole brain on.

The antagonistic system to the RAS is the DICTS (diffusely inhibitory caudate tissue system). The caudate nucleus is the second largest area in the brain. Once again, the inhibitory process begins in the cortex, and caudate inhibition balances reticular excitation.

The human thought process is horizontal and circular (engrams). The servo loop of the RAS to DICTS is a vertical loop. The cortex possesses the ability to communicate with the thalamus. When a hypnotist produces a whole-body catalepsy, suspending the body between two chairs with the heels on one and the head on the other, the thalamus has interpreted cortical language thus: the body is rigid and stiff like a bar of steel.

There are essentially three fiber systems in the brain:
1. The ascending projection fibers
2. The transhemispheric association fibers
3. The intrahemispheric fibers

Meditation, a cortically induced state, essentially turns off the projection fibers, which normally input information from the outside. Meditation, hypnosis, and biofeedback all have in common cortical associations with slowed brain wave activity.

Behavior is ostensibly a stimulus response. When brain wave activity is plotted on a graph measuring behavior/response on one axis and mobilization/arousal on the other, an inverted U function is derived:

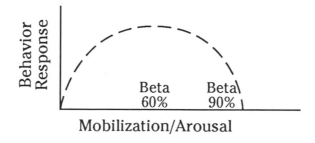

Thus, too much stimuli will produce the same results as too little with respect to response and arousal.

Perhaps another way of looking at this will make this concept clearer. There are four levels of brain wave activity:

1. Beta—full waking to super-excitation conscious state
2. Alpha—twilight zone associated with hypnosis, meditation, deep relaxation, and rem sleep cycles
3. Theta—deep sleep state
4. Delta—comatose state

Each level of brain wave activity corresponds to a level of personal consciousness which interprets stimuli producing not only behavioral but physiological responses. As models:

Brain Associations:

Level 1: Medulla spinal column
Level 2: Hypothalamus
Level 3: Cortex

SELF-RESPONSIBLE MAN

Now, all of this adds up to the suggestion that man has the ability to interpret (or reinterpret) stimuli and thus control and manage behavior or response (nothing really new about this). Thus, man need not be viewed as a victim of his environment and enculturation; rather, he should be viewed as a child on a maturation curve, learning management skills that produce self-responsibility. As victim, man has little or no role in his destiny; as a self-responsible cocreator he assumes control of who and what he may become. Our learning curve, or maturation process, with

59

its Freudian physics and traditional psychological heritage, may be modeled like this:

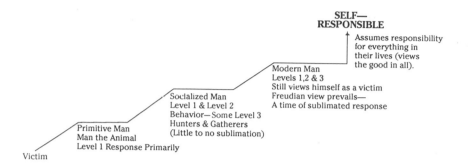

The self-responsible person is accepting and forgiving. The victim needs (perceives) acceptance and forgiveness. The victim's greatest fear is absolute, total rejection, so his behavior is sublimated, modified, and selected (chosen) to seek and find approval and acceptance while minimizing significant rejection, which arises out of his perception of self and significant others or their surrogates. The victim is condition/response oriented to victimhood. The lens of the victim's perception is such that it reinforces the condition/response victim mechanism. Whether an issue of health or the subject of relationships, the victim is under siege by stimuli not under his control. On the other hand, the self-responsible person accepts that he chose whatever dysfunction he has and sets about learning from it.

It is my opinion that scripted in the biocomputer (brain) are victim scenarios that become self-fulfilling expectations generating everything from psychophysical dysfunction to externally perceived "threatening" stimuli (not the saber-tooth tiger kind) and that what indeed occurs with subliminal communication is a systematic desensitization of fear threats together with the installation of a new lens to interpret the world. In other words, the mechanic should now be in place to see as at least one possibility the alternative that man is what he expects (believes) himself to be, empowered by the degree of responsibility he accepts for himself. Perhaps, in more than a metaphorical sense, as Bach said in

Jonathan Livingston Seagull, "Argue for limitations and they're yours."

On the basis of sublimation man has projected himself for the purpose of acceptance and alienated himself in doing so. Thus he has stood for the past several centuries as a mere shadow of himself, so afraid of rejection that he has rejected himself. The bottom line is that he cannot possibly find acceptance, for he has lost himself.

In man's maturation process, interpreting stimuli begins in the cradle. One day the same outcries that fostered care (clean diapers, a loving touch, and nourishment) produce pain—or worse, nothing. The cries go unanswered. The helpless infant exaggerates the need by crying louder and longer. Adjustments, perceptual based behavior, condition/response training has begun. To this extent Freud was right; he accurately envisioned the still helpless infant (victim) in the adult.

CHAPTER SEVEN

SUBLIMINAL TECHNOLOGY AND THE INDUSTRY IN SUBLIMINALS

*The ultimate value of science is the
test the consumer applies. —Roy Bey*

A REVIEW OF THE TECHNOLOGY

Before we go further, a quick review of technology may assist us. The two senses most often appealed to subliminally are the aural and the visual senses. Generally, videosubliminal stimuli is generated in one of three ways:

1. Slide insertion.
2. Candlepower ratio levels
3. Tachistoscope projection

A number of modalities are involved in audiosubliminal projection as well. Perhaps the best known is Becker's black box, the device that Professor Becker patented in 1969. Essentially, the most popular methods are:

1. Becker's black box
2. Psychoacoustical concealment
3. Back-masking, or metacontrast
4. White-sound masking
5. Electronic synchronization

Several methods are derived from each of these five, and there is some overlapping, as further discussion will reveal. There is also great debate over the speed of messages, as in time-compressed modalities, and the frequency bands used to modulate the subliminal, especially where inexpensive players are used to review the content.

The commercial marketplace is full of "snake oil" salespeople. Audiosubliminals have created a new industry in America, selling instant fixes for everything from poverty to obesity. Many of these companies are peddling absolute panaceas in their claims, implicitly if not explicitly. Some have adopted the old "more is better" mentality, and there appears to be open competition over who can get the most affirmations on a single tape.

In my opinion, subliminal self-help is not only here to stay but in the near future will represent a preferred method for effecting beneficial change. It is important to understand that just as subliminals are *not* the invisible and therefore nonexistent-yet-pretended-to-be-perceived emperor's clothes, they are also *not* a panacea. There are definite limitations and even contraindications to their use. It is the informed consumer who eventually will decide what companies will remain in business when the initial awe of new technology is replaced by consumer awareness.

Manufacturers and Technology

Becker's black box processes spoken words into music by simply averaging the volume levels of the music and producing the spoken word as a subliminal slightly beneath the music volume. Ordinarily, tracings of this process show the following:

Music level

Subliminal level

Since the process and its various derivations use averages, however, it is not at all uncommon to produce the following tracing:

Music

Subliminal

It can be seen that the subliminal content may thus become audible or semiaudible during part of the programming.

A very close cousin to Becker's process is one developed by Dr. Louis Romberg, a native of East Germany, who began researching subliminal communication in the early 1960s. Romberg's device was installed in a Canadian tire store in Toronto that offered a line of general hardware. The reported result was that employee productivity went up and thefts went down considerably.

Still another process that is derived from Becker's technology is the property of the Institute of Human Development and is used to produce a commercial line of audiotapes.

Psychoacoustical concealment can be accomplished in a number of ways, one of which is to harmonize voice frequency with primary sound output. Sometimes the voice is made to sound like an instrument and sometimes like "pink" or "gray" sound, which is simply background sound such as the "swooshing" of a gentle wind.

One company reformatting voice frequencies to conceal them in the music is Valley of the Sun. The creator of Valley of the Sun, Richard Sutphen, asserts that when his effort to acquire rights to Becker's black box was broken off, he engaged sound engineers in California to develop the process. Sutphen felt that the ease with which they came up with the process was frightening, especially in view of the fact that the subliminal content cannot then be rediscovered even with the use of sophisticated equipment, including the parametric analyzer.

In effect, "white" sound mixing and acoustical concealment are nearly the same. The difference is that white sound contains all audible sound frequencies. Therefore, the voice track used to produce the subliminal either must be matched with specific frequencies used by musical instruments, or lowered slightly below the white sound background (usually the sound of ocean surf).

Back-masking usually is accomplished in frequency mixing; however, in this instance the audio track of spoken messages is reversed, or played backwards. Ultrahigh and extra low frequencies can also be incorporated in any of these formats. The silent dog whistle is a simple example of a frequency not consciously perceived by the human ear and yet verifiably perceived by the human's unconscious or subconscious or somatic processes.

Means to create audiosubliminal recordings range from the sophisticated digital recording equipment to the "home-made" version described in *Subliminal Communication*. Some of these processes include multilayer, multifrequency, voice compression, time compression, and the list goes on. Now let us examine what scientific findings regarding technology exist and then return to the claims made by subliminal product manufacturers.

SCIENCE AND THE MANUFACTURER'S TECHNOLOGY

A French study conducted by Borgeat and Pannetier examined the usefulness of averaging electrodermal potential responses for purposes of research connected to subliminal auditory perception. The study had eighteen female subjects exposed to emotional, neutral, and 1000 Hz tone of auditory stimulation, with the stimuli repeated six times at three intensities. Analysis of electrodermal potential responses indicated that "the number of responses was related to the *emotionality* of subliminal stimuli presented at detection threshold but not at 10 decibels under it." (My emphasis added.) (Borgeat, Pannetier, 1982.)

A study conducted at St. John's University investigated subliminal and supraliminal accessory stimulation on two dynamic perceptual illusions. Eighteen undergraduates were used as subjects. The findings showed that "only the most extreme subliminal stimulation (30 db below threshold) was effective, significantly increasing the number of illusory experiences." (Zenhausern, Ciaiola, Pompo, 1973.)

Psychophysiological responses to masked auditory verbal stimuli were studied by H. Louis of the Psychiatric Research Center at Lafontain Hospital in Montreal, Canada. Louis increased intensities in auditory verbal stimuli using twenty twenty-one- to thirty-year-old healthy women. "Verbal stimuli, masked by a 40 db white noise, were presented to the 5 (subjects) at increasing intensities by increments of 5 db starting at 0 db. At each increment, frontal EMK, skin conductance, and heart rates were recorded." Results demonstrated psychophysiological responses to stimuli presented below the thresholds of detection and identification. (Borgeat, Elie, Chaloult, Chabot, 1985.)

In another study conducted at St. John's University, Robert Zenhausern and Karen Hansen examined the differential effect of subliminal and supraliminal accessory stimulation on task components in problem solving. Utilizing the Stencil Design Test on thirty-five male graduates and undergraduates, the experiment showed that subjects presented stimuli at "30 db below threshold and 35 db above threshold resulted in performance decrement, while 10 db below threshold and 60 db above threshold led to facilitation." (Zenhausern, Hansen, 1974.)

Gerald Murch of Portland State College published a study regarding temporal gradients of responses to subliminal stimuli in the *Psychological Record*. Murch's results indicated "increased response probabilities after delays of 1, 100, and 250 msec." Murch used a tachistoscope to present the visual stimuli. (Zenhausern, Pompo, Ciaiola, 1974.)

In another article by Murch, which appeared in the *Journal of Applied Psychology*, a set of conditions for the consistent recovery of a subliminal stimulus were presented based on an earlier study. Murch used three experimental groups of ten subjects, each group with a corresponding control group, to present mathematical problems in a tachistoscope as a supraliminal stimulus. The experimental groups were given subliminal answers to the problems. "Group 1 attempted to solve the problems, Group 2 to guess at the answers, and Group 3 to select their answers from dual possibilities on a given list. A significant tendency was found in Groups 1 and 2 to repeat various subliminally projected digits in their answers, without the answers directly affecting their computational processes. Group 3 selected the projected answers significantly over the correct answers." Murch presented the subliminal at the exposure speed of 5/1000 of a second. (Murch, 1965.)

Anthony Marcel conducted five thorough experiments on visual masking and work recognition whose findings were published in *Cognitive Psychology*. Marcel concluded: "It is proposed that central pattern masking has little effect on visual processing itself (while peripheral energy masking does), but affects availability of records of the results of those processes to consciousness. Perceptual processing itself is unconscious and automatically proceeds to all levels of analysis and redescription available to the perceiver." (1983.)

TRADE SECRETS

In all of these studies, either the subthreshold level was determined as part of the experiment or a previously determined subthreshold level was applied, and that was the experiment. Science and business separate themselves on a number of criteria, but none more flagrantly than in the opposing attitudes toward verifiability and trade secrets.

Subliminal product manufacturers for the most part are commercial businesses, and trade secrets do not provide a fertile field for science to investigate. Where science discloses methodology as important to verifiability, industry prefers to offer only results. Still, industry wants science to support its claims. It is no wonder that the response from science is often "there is no evidence."

Manufacturers of subliminals make a lot of claims, just as any sales-built organization is inclined to do, whether it is used cars or pharmacology. It is important for the claims to represent reputable information, or the consumer soon shuts down the claimant's business. Let us review some of the claims being made by subliminal manufacturers, who presently have no real policing body, though efforts are currently underway within the industry to create a panel that will approve general methodologies and assertions for consumer awareness and self-policing.

Most manufacturers of subliminal products are very responsible. Still, there are often claims made that seem to have little if any scientific substantiation. In a phone conversation I had with a manufacturer in New York, I was told of a technology he was employing to create subliminal audiocassettes with one million affirmations per sixty-minute recording. In a followup conversation with this manufacturer, he explained his process and stated that if the conscious mind could hear the subliminal content of his programs, what it would discern is "just noise." In my work *Subliminal Communication* I refer to million-message strategies as belonging to "more is better mentality." The research generally favors real-time languaging; however, since *Subliminal Communication* was published, at least one study has surfaced indicating comprehension of speech-compressed subliminal stimuli. (We'll discuss this and other speech-compressed studies in more detail later in this chapter.) Formerly I have held that somewhere in the marketing strategy of some companies is the idea that more programs can be sold, and sold for higher prices, if more affirmations are included on each tape. The pitch usually goes like this:

> All of one's life negative messaging has accumulated in the subconscious mind. This negative content outnumbers the positive input by at least ten to one. In order to truly accept one's positive self and real abilities and express one's potential, one must outweigh the negative with positive. One must believe in himself! [Up to this point the statements are generally accurate.] In order to make this possible, hundreds of thousands, even millions, of messages are on each of our (ABC companies') programs. The quantity outweighs the old negative programming rapidly at this rate. Overnight you will see a vast improvement [and so forth].

There is a great controversy among manufacturers of subliminals about the million-message idea. Consumers seem to like the idea, and that creates competitive pressures on manufacturers. A recent phone call from James Griswold of Love Tapes, a reliable and reputable company, brought to my attention a company I had previously complimented on their programs. Mr. Griswold told me that this company was now using time- or speech-compression methods. At the time I complimented the manufacturer, speech-compression was not part of their product. Still, Mr. Griswold naturally associated my earlier compliment with this company's present advertisements regarding hundreds of thousands of affirmations.

Mr. Griswold simply asked, "Is there any evidence that more messages (the hundred thousand variety) is preferred to the real time subliminal presentation method?" Mr. Griswold went on to say that Love Tapes was interested in the quality of their product first and genuinely desired to provide their consumers with the best possible product.

My answer to Mr. Griswold was a firm *no*. With the exception set forth earlier, there is no evidence that I am familiar with. Nonetheless, one manufacturer's literature states that his tapes have been scientifically proven, and this manufacturer's advisory board is a collection of experts highly credible in their fields. Still, in my opinion, there are two questions that need to be asked about the million-message claim: first, does the brain possess the capability to perceive stimuli at this rate? second, if it perceives it, is it meaningful? The answer to the first is, certainly, and the response to the second is, probably not any more meaningful than sixty cycles of electricity coursing through the wiring in your home.

The brain technically perceives and processes an incredible amount of information. Internal and external stimuli are continually and simultaneously inputted. The RAS (reticular activating system) is on and the thalamus is mediating, to use a grossly simplified metaphor. Nonmeaningful input is ignored, if not essentially discarded. Our bodies are a constant noise as our blood pumps and our organs function, and this somatic information is being monitored in the brain. We are unaware of these processes until there is a malfunction. Suddenly one day thalamus tells cortex that the heart is beating 140 beats per minute, and we hear our bodies.

Some people will wake in the middle of the night when their electricity goes out. Others are so accustomed to silence that the sound of electricity disturbs them. The valid question then is not whether the brain perceives, but is what it perceives meaningful?

The negative messaging one has accumulated over a lifetime has its power because it was delivered in a meaningful way. Behavior is not just a matter of information processing, like electromagnetic smog; it is more involved with the interpretation of the input data than with the data itself.

Language is a learned skill. It is somewhat like the screen language of the computer. Archetypes in this analogy can be seen as the mechanical language underlying the visible on the screen. (See the examples below.) Learned language (English vocabulary) connects to mechanical archetypes. The archetypes imbue language with its flavor.

MECHANICAL LANGUAGE

Example 1

```
D:b■t4 \ hH■
X 1 h@■
xF■'■ 8 7M!
B?£
    5  r.u'
■$_<Ft        :~■4      M!M F■j■_
F■i■ F■f■ F■'k¶ F■f■ F■'F■i■ F■j■ k '_

J£Bb  ZBR<$+B∨Dpt_3@l■S'#■#■■-$%  /¹
■:J■4
```

SCREEN LANGUAGE

Example 2

```
date
time
echo off
prompt $p$g
verify on
path c:\dos
vscreen
```

To demonstrate how learned language connects to mechanical archetypes, I have used successfully an easy experiment on hundreds of people. Simply have the person imagine a bright white light coming down, entering his body at the top of his head, filling his entire body, and then radiating outward two or three feet. (All experience feelings of warmth, security, and comfort.) Then ask him to do the same thing with gray. (All experience eerie or discomforting feelings.)

In my opinion, one would be better served with a subliminal program in Russian (assuming you are not fluent in Russian) than with a highly time-compressed or rapidly sped-up speech program, to say nothing of the million-message stuff. If the conscious mind could not understand a learned, conscious skill (language), there is little evidence to support that the subconscious can magically translate it. By the same token, reversing language as in metacontrasting techniques can generally be interpreted by the conscious mind if the mind is allowed access to the content spoken slowly. Mild speech compression likewise can be made intelligible by the conscious mind. In my opinion, the truth of the matter is not yet known as an absolute, but it probably will be found to function somewhat in a direct proportion, that is, as the conscious intelligibility diminishes, the program's effectiveness likewise diminishes. I do not believe what a manufacturer of subliminals told me recently, that the subconscious mind translates a language it has never learned, whether it is English spoken too rapidly or Hebrew to an English-only speaker. It is noteworthy and appropriate to cite at this point the textbook estimates based on theoretical limits of the rate of information processing in the auditory system. The maximum capacity of the human ear is thereby calculated to be as follows:

> 8,000 bits/sec - random sound
> 10,000 bits/sec - loud sounds
> 50 bits/sec - language
> 70 bits/sec - music
> based on 150,000 word vocabulary and a speaking rate of 300 words/min. (Wolman, 1971.)

There are essentially four ways to put more messages in a subliminal audio presentation:
1. Time compression
2. Sped-up speech
3. Multilayering or multitracking
4. Multifrequencing

TIME COMPRESSION AND SPED-UP SPEECH

Time compression is a digital process of removing spacing between sounds, syllables, and words. This compression can be done to some extent and the content still be intelligible. Remember, however, speech is often more meaningful because of its meter

71

or rhythm and, like music, when spacing is removed altogether, what remains is continuous noise.

Some right brain research suggests that verbal messaging may have increased value if sung. In some subjects where corpus callosum fiber has been separated from the two brain hemispheres (split-brain studies), speaking a word to the right brain could lead to the identification of an object but not to the ability to articulate the word, whereas singing the word allowed for semantic construction.

Sped-up speech is the simple process of recording verbal content at, say, 15/16 inches per second (ips) and then playing it back at 15 ips. The old "Chipmunk" recordings were a simple 2 to 1, not 16 to 1, and it is difficult for me to imagine taking too seriously anything the Chipmunks could have said. Still, there is intelligibility at rates of 2 and 3 to 1. Nevertheless, findings in one study conducted by Vaugn Kaser did suggest the possibility that the unconscious/preconscious mind is able to perceive a verbal recording at speeds that the conscious cannot understand. The message in that study was sung and then sped up. The effect of the auditory subliminal message was measured in imagery and dreams as produced by the subjects in pre- and posttest drawings. (Kaser, 1986.)

Still, Dr. Paul Tuthill of Mind Communications took the question regarding the claim of one hundred thousand messages per hour to R. M. Shultz and Associates, a prominent electronics design and research firm in the Midwest. Shultz, an electronics engineer, responded:

> There is a definite limit to the number of voice affirmations which can be recorded on an audiotape. The limitations are forced due to band width restrictions of both the audio equipment and the human ear. Six seconds of normal speech data compressed six times has a band width requirement (without loss of comprehension) of 15 KH2. This implies that a conventional quality tape recorder is capable of approximately 3,600 affirmations in a one-hour period. At this rate the audio reproduction capabilities of both the recording tape and the tape recorder itself are pushed to their limits. (Tuthill, 1988.)

Shultz continues to assert that claims of the one-hundred-thousand messages variety are deceptive; however, he has qualified his statement by defining the physical limitations of tapes and equipment according to limits of "comprehension." Obviously, this begs the question. Although thirty-six hundred affirmations may be optimal according to this model, simply adding echo to the voice tracks being mixed as subliminal messages would "deepen," or multiply, the content by four or five times without stretching the physical limitations of tape and equipment.

Numerous other studies contradict Kaser's experiment, and his findings have not been replicated. More important, other scientific findings regarding subliminal communication used speech presented at normal rates of speed. Everything cited in this work or that I have been able to find is representative of intelligible verbal audible or visual (verbal and pictorial) content. Additionally, my own research and data collection suggest that speech delivered subliminally at high rates of speed, which necessarily moves the speech into higher frequencies that sometimes sound like a high pitched squeal, produces more headaches than any other subjective or objective measurable effect.

A study conducted by E. A. Kostandov of the Central Scientific Research Institute of Legal Psychiatry in Moscow, USSR, examining the effect of emotional content on the recognition threshold of words resulted in the conclusion that emotional words contained higher verbal recognition thresholds. Kostandov delivered words subliminally to subjects at the rate of one every five seconds. (Kostandov, 1977.)

According to the United States Army Research Institute for the Behavioral and Social Sciences publication, the awareness threshold is significant where speech rate is concerned. In Technical Paper 297 the findings indicate that in comparing sped-up speech with compressed speech, a significantly higher threshold exists with compressed speech. This indicates at the very least that the threshold reflects intelligibility. A second experiment published in this same paper measured comprehension test scores as correlated to threshold values. Findings indicated low correlation. The results were interpreted to mean that the threshold reflects information processing involving the perception of the potential for interpretation at an intermediate level or comprehension rather than a complete act of comprehension. (deHaan, 1978.)

Gail Hardy and D. Legge of University College in London, England, studied changes in sensory thresholds relating to emotionally meaningful subliminal stimulation through both visual and auditory presentations. They concluded that emotional stimulation is mediated centrally. (Hardy, 1968.) (We will discuss emotive content in more detail in the next chapter.)

MULTILAYERING AND MULTIFREQUENCING

Multilayering is a recording technique in which tracks are layered together; multifrequencing is a recording technique in which tracks are mixed at differing frequencies. Two constraints are noteworthy here. First, there is a difference between multilayered sound engineering beauty, and garble. Second, the human range of audibility is less than what a sound engineer could produce by multifrequencing; and magnetic tape possesses recording range capabilities far beyond what the ordinary cassette player can produce.

Now, imagine some company producing a subliminal audiocassette tape using time compression or sped-up speech with multilayering and multifrequencing techniques, and doing so at the rate of speech and number of variables necessary to get one million affirmations on a sixty-minute program. This is mind-boggling, to say the least. It is no wonder that some reputable scientists exposed only to this merchandising method say "hogwash!"

OTHER MARKETING STRATEGIES

Another marketing strategy that disturbs me is the magic and mystery marketeers. There is nothing mysterious about subliminal communication, nor is there anything magical. At best, subliminal products are antidotes for self-poisoning or self-limiting beliefs.

Some companies insist that their subliminal verbal message content remain secret, asserting that the power only works if you are consciously unaware of the messages. They argue that conscious awareness provides the conscious mind with the ability to reject the messaging. It is so powerful that it bypasses the conscious mind unless the conscious mind knows what the message is? Nonsense! Except in the instance of the symbiotic message, which is discussed in detail in the next chapter, there is absolutely no evidence, including elementary logic, to support such a statement.

74

One way, however, to avoid being held accountable for content is simply not to publish it. This frightens me. Recently I reviewed some subliminal dialogues written and produced by a respectable psychologist. Here are some actual affirmations from two different titles:

Quitting Smoking

Smoke is poison.

Cigarette smoke poisons the body.

Male Sensuality

God loves sex.

Fucking is good.

Now, since four in five smokers who give up their cigarettes restart the habit, what expectation is there in the subconscious mind as a residual from the "Quitting Smoking" program? Obviously, the smoker expects to die, and guess what happens. Next, is intimacy about fucking? Is sensuality served with the phrase "God loves sex"? Any kind of sex?

These examples provide another good reason that a consumer should require, as a condition of purchase, a printed copy of the subliminal verbal content. Since subliminals are a powerful tool, verbal content is of critical importance. (For more information regarding affirmation usage in subliminal applications, see *Subliminal Communication: Emperor's Clothes or Panacea?*)

Most major manufacturers of subliminals will provide scripts with their programs. Many package them inside with their cassettes or software. Concerned manufacturers usually happily volunteer information about their recording procedure—how their products are produced. It is my experience that the more reliable the manufacturers, the more open they are about what they are doing. Most producers of subliminals are working diligently to cooperate with science, raise the consumer level of awareness, and establish a solid basis for any and all claims. In my opinion, the industry deserves praise for its overall efforts and level of integrity. (For a list of subliminal suppliers, see page 141.)

CHAPTER EIGHT

In Search of Consciousness

A thought is an idea in transit.
—Pythagoras

Conscious or Unconscious

A case could be made for the idea that subliminal awareness originated before consciousness became articulate. Ancient mystical writings, together with commentaries upon these writings by a veritable who's who from the science community throughout history, have alleged that consciousness exists within a larger body of consciousness; that thoughts are energy transmissions and the mind (individualized and as a whole) is a transceiver, sending and receiving. Without this assumption, the evolution of consciousness or its artifact, intelligence (knowledge as opposed to wisdom), would have been experientially limited.

But imagine, if you will, a time when men spoke not of themselves or, perhaps, spoke not at all; a time when man spoke no words nor heard words per se, for words did not exist; a time when the individual did not recognize the nature of individuality; a time when all worked in unison for the benefit of one and all, much in the way an ant colony provides for self by first accepting duty, responsibility, and action on behalf of all; a time when the gods spoke directly in orchestrating all activities; a time when, like the queen ant's, all knowledge was noetic; a time when knowing was an inner prompting, an intuitive guidance, an expression of instinctual urge, a sharing of thought without words, or a vision of pictures portraying purpose and need; a time when a sort of telepathic community of man experienced without thinking, knew without intellectualizing, witnessed without testifying, served without even the notion of service, or sensed without the discrimination of the five senses as separately sensing.

Can you imagine such a time on earth many, many centuries ago? Can you find deep down in your mind images, visions, memories of such a time? Have you ever experienced a knowing or a feeling of knowing that defied the evidences of the senses or the intellect? Have you ever felt an inner prompting? How about a feeling of deja vu? Have you experienced any form of paranormal knowing? Literally everyone, at some time in his life, has received some form of inner nonverbal guidance, maybe in his dreams or perhaps out of the blue. Is it then difficult to imagine such a world where the analog *I* or words per se did not exist? I think not.

But what if such a world really existed, antedating recorded history as we know it? A world where all for one and one for all were not words, just natural relationships. Could this have been the kind of knowing mystical writings proffer?

Was man plagued not by the ability to think, but by the verbalization of his thoughts? Did his words become things that separated him not just from his world and others, but ultimately from himself and therefore from reality? Did his gods abandon him or confuse him so that he might learn the value of knowing? Was there, metaphorically speaking, a tower of Babel from which man was given not only different languages but language itself to punish him for some transgression? Or, for that matter, was language given for some other reason, including the whims of his gods?

Is it possible that, as the Garden of Eden parable teaches, it was indeed the fruit of the tree of *knowledge* that cast man out and away from the presence of God? Was it a self-imposed ostracism or castigation, a time when man began denying his gods and worshipping his intellect?

Are the voices from within a paranormal activity, a birthright given by God, or a function of maladaptive psychology? Julian Jaynes, in his marvelous work *The Origin of Consciousness in the Breakdown of the Bicameral Mind*, relegates these voices to the realm of schizophrenia. But let's not get the cart before the horse; Jaynes's work is amply worthy of review.

To begin, Jaynes sets up a timetable tracing the evolution of consciousness to the creation and use of the analog *I*. Strictly speaking within the Jaynes paradigm, man spoke only to himself and his god (or gods) until his consciousness had sufficiently evolved to communicate with others. Those who did not evolve were destroyed, a sort of survival of the fittest according to the desire and perception of the fittest groups.

Jaynes schematizes and documents his argument this way:

> At a point in the history of man, civilizations existed without consciousness, at least without oral consciousness or consciousness of consciousness. "Subjective conscious mind is an analogy of what is called the real world. It is built up with vocabulary or a lexical field whose terms are all metaphors or analogs of behavior in the physical world. Its reality is of the same order as mathematics. It allows us to shortcut behavioral processes and arrive at more adequate decisions. Like mathematics, it is an operator rather than a thing or repository. And it is intimately bound up with volition and decision. (1976).

To understand this, you must first understand *consciousness.* Jaynes treats this subject marvelously in the first chapter of his work, and I treat it in my *Exclusively Fabricated Illusions.* But for the benefit of those who have read neither of these accounts or any of many other fine works on the subject, *consciousness* will be examined here before we advance any further.

AWARENESS

The nature of consciousness, that is, your awareness of unique you, has been the subject of controversy since man first postulated his independent self as acting and interacting in the world. Without critical thought, the average individual is likely to categorize consciousness as simply "being awake." Metaphysicians historically deal with consciousness in its higher form as an altered state of consciousness that somehow transcends the personal ego consciousness but remains either as ineffable experience consciousness or consciousness of higher consciousness, never treating what constitutes *real* consciousness.

It is important that we understand consciousness with its various attending degrees and elements if we are to approach any theory proposing its evolution or operation—conscious, preconscious/subliminal conscious, subconscious/unconscious operation. In other words, consciousness is not merely a state of being awake or being aware of consciousness, but rather it is an integration of levels of consciousness and perhaps what Jung referred to as collective consciousness, or the collective unconscious. In my opinion it is an unfolding (self-realizing) and addictive collective consciousness manifested in a particular form—and here I am using the Platonic distinction of particular and form, where the form, say, is chairness, and the particular is a specific chair, such as a Boston rocker. Obviously, all chairs are not alike, and yet the construct of chairness serves to facilitate the communication and understanding or agreement of what constitutes a particular chair. If this seems confusing, try answering the question: what is consciousness without an object?

Consciousness Defined?

To better approach a definition of consciousness, let us examine what is usually thought of as the meaning of consciousness.

It took mankind years to come to grips with distinctions among conscious levels of the mind. Centuries went by, flooding literature with truths, before man accepted the existence of the dark and mysterious unconscious mind that operates on many different levels. It was nearly a century after the birth of psychoanalytic theory that man legitimized the study of his "sixth sense" and institutions began to offer curricula culminating ultimately in some degree or diploma in parapsychology. Any definition of *consciousness* must now also include the componential ingredient referred to herein as "sixth sense" in order to properly incorporate the various phenomena somehow actuated into our realization of what we can say consciousness is or is not. (There exists a

79

high correlation between the conditions for perception of subliminal stimuli and psi-related phenomena. See chapter 9.)

REACTIVITY

Consciousness is not reactivity. Reactivity is an unconscious reaction to a stimuli. The classical Pavlovian conditioned response is a good example of this. We are constantly reacting to conditions in our internal and external environments without conscious awareness of them. For example, our bodies are constantly adjusting to the food we eat, the air we breathe, and the thoughts we think. While we may think of something perhaps erotic or frightening, we are nevertheless not consciously causing the sympathetic or parasympathetic nervous system to produce the corresponding physiological responses. Even when we are aware of the correlation between thought and physiological responses, we are not consciously thinking of the reactivity alone but rather of the association. In fact, the more aware of the association we become in an analytical way, the less likely the intensity of the immediate response in the reactive relationship will exist.

When the reactivity is from the external, the same rules apply. Take, for instance, the perception of all or any of what is around us. You may or may not be conscious of many things you have seen a multitude of times. I am reminded here of the incident from the movie *First Monday in October*, in which Walter Matthau was asked by his estranged wife to describe the wallpaper in his home. Just as Matthau had limited his conscious selection to preclude the observance of wallpaper, so does our conscious state rather arbitrarily select that which we will become conscious of, but we seem to do so by operation of some unconscious modality priority. (Defense mechanisms, for example.) That is, if we become conscious of that which we are not conscious of, then we become conscious of that which we were previously unconscious of, although we were, nonetheless, conscious. In that sense, consciousness becomes a much smaller aspect of our mental activity than we can be conscious of, for "we cannot be conscious of what we are not conscious of." (Jaynes, 1976.)

A Memory Slate

"All men by nature desire to know," in the words of Aristotle (Ross and Kaplan, 1970), and "to know" presupposes consciousness. Aristotle went on to postulate what has been known for centuries as the "blank mind" metaphor. In the seventeenth century, John Locke again popularized this concept with his tabula rasa theory of consciousness. In the seventies of this century, J. Krishnamurti, in a lecture delivered on the campus of the University of California at Berkeley, elaborated what has become a very popular theory of consciousness that emphasizes the recording, cameralike nature of the mind. Krishnamurti presented the construct that the idea of freedom of thought is sheer nonsense, that the ability to express whatever you choose is illusion. Thought is not free, for it responds from memory. (1972.)

Now, if consciousness is a memory slate, are we conscious of the consciousness? Are there not many things of which we have unconscious recollections? Professionally, I have used hypnosis forensically on victims and witnesses to get at memory concealed from the conscious mind. Is an unconscious memory therefore a part of consciousness? How many of us are guilty of partial amnesia, suppressing rejected memories for the sake of our psychological well-being and simply forgetting material that ranges in variety from a best friend in the first grade to rote-core memory work in preparation for an examination? Is this all consciousness, or are we committed to an unconscious consciousness? Jaynes says, "Conscious retrospection is not the retrieval of images, but the retrieval of what you have been conscious of before, and the reworking of these elements into rational or plausible patterns." (1976.)

Clearly, consciousness is more than (and at the same time, less than) that represented in the "blank mind" theory or any derivation of it. This definition only approximates a hypothesis that, when tested, leaves us far short of an axiomatic understanding.

Can we say that consciousness is the interaction of everything aforestated and that evidence of it and its function is a priori? After all, I am writing, you are reading, and presumably some mental processes are occurring in this exchange. Can we say that *this* is consciousness? If we do, are we also committed logically to

81

conclude that consciousness is evidenced by learning, by grasping concepts, by reasoning and thinking?

Ah yes, you may emphatically say. But consciousness is not necessary to thinking, to learning, or to constructing concepts. Where concepts are concerned, consider this: Has anyone ever seen *the* chair or only *a* chair? Remember the Platonic example earlier of chairness and the Boston rocker? Now, when you examine this issue, recognize that all anyone has ever witnessed is the particular. The form eludes reference except by orientation to the particular. Consider the form of danger or of sanctuary. Anyone who has spent time with nature knows that animals and even insects are familiar with these forms and in some instances seem to sense both simultaneously without apparent stimuli. So is consciousness the awareness of the form, or concept. Is the consciousness of a tree hibernating for the winter different from the consciousness of a bear or a homo sapien sapien? Alas, what we want to mean by consciousness is different somehow from that which we would attribute to the oak or to the grizzly. In fact, the psychologist would say that these are root concepts and are fundamentally prior to experience. These root concepts are essentially a part of the neurological basis of aptitudes. Thus we must conclude that concepts are essentially either a function of language or something quite unlike what we originally wanted to say was consciousness.

LEARNING AND THINKING

What about learning and thinking? First, let us discuss learning. We alluded earlier to Pavlovian condition-response learning. You ring a bell, and because for 140 times or so the bell's ringing is associated with the dispensation of food, salivation occurs. That is definitely a learning process, but is it consciousness? No. In fact, science has learned that conscious awareness of condition-response techniques actually inhibits the learning process. We have all read about or studied the proverbial "maze bright" rat sufficiently to know that an overstimulated bright rat suddenly becomes dull indeed. Is this an example of conscious interference again? How about those often taken for granted sensory-motor skills that all of us have to some extent? When I become conscious of every motion of my pen as I write, the errors become exceedingly frequent. When the trained athlete becomes conscious of each movement, so goes inversely his ability to perform that movement. Is this the conscious mind interfering? Is consciousness necessary to learning? Perhaps not, you say, at least where motor skills are involved; but how about all that learning of the mental, the abstract to the mathematical, the implicit to the implied?

That brings us to thinking and solution learning. As implied before, solution learning can be synthetic to a conditioned stimuli and hence is not consciousness at all. Thinking, on the other hand, appears to have the solution to this quandary regarding consciousness—or does it? Psychologists tell us that, to the contrary, it appears thinking is automatic. "Another way of saying it is that one does one's thinking before one knows what one is to think about." (Jaynes, 1976.) The important part is the instruction, which allows the whole business to go off automatically.

This term has been shortened by Jaynes to the term *struction*, which is meant to have the connotation of both *instruction* and *construction*. "Thinking then is not conscious. Rather, it is an automatic process following a struction and the materials on which the struction is to operate." (Jaynes, 1976.)

All right then, you might ask, what about the propensity of rational intellect known as reason? Certainly this is consciousness! Only word games could refute this most elemental evidence of reasoning. After all, all logic systems, all knowledge per se, all technology vociferously pronounce the existence of reason and therefore intellect and, obviously, consciousness.

This is really a two-part issue. Reasoning of many varieties occurs, and one of these is a system of inference. What exactly is inference? If a child is viciously bitten by the first dog he or she comes in contact with, will the child automatically infer that all dogs are dangerous? If the same child wanders into the neighborhood to be traumatized by another dog that is only halted from mauling the child by a chain fastened securely around its neck, will the child surely conclude that all dogs are evil and dangerous? At some point, with only this negative reference reinforcement, will the child develop a phobia? Even as an adult, and with full awareness of the source of the phobia, will it ever be entirely shed? Is this conscious reasoning? How does reasoning control

83

conscious fear? Was it necessary to become conscious before fear entered the scene?

Another form of reasoning is that of value judgments of our feelings or perceptions about others' feelings, perceptions, and character. Psychologists infer that "these are clearly the result of automatic inferences by our nervous system in which consciousness is not only unnecessary, but, as we have seen in the performance of motor skills, would probably hinder the process." (Jaynes, 1976.)

Reason by inference again? Category reasoning? Experiential reasoning? Generalization? There is nothing extraordinary here—all higher vertebrates possess this faculty. Is this consciousness?

How about empirical reasoning? Literature abounds with tales of creative genius. Flowing through nearly all of them is inspiration. As inspirational thought suddenly and overwhelmingly consumes the conscious, sometimes forcing itself upon its author and sometimes creating such jubilant excitement as to cause a cautious Einstein to hold his razor with two hands while shaving so as to avoid cutting himself when inspiration descended. What person has not had a seemingly unsolvable problem, the solution to which just "popped" into his head? Inspiration is so common to the species that little ado attends it unless it is of the spiritual or genius category.

So, is the highest of all reasoning factors, the inspiration behind the solution, an unconscious occasion? This too is neither what we want in our meaning of consciousness nor what we mean for our definition to communicate.

What then is consciousness, and where does it come from? Are we capable of comprehending an unconscious civilization such as Jaynes suggests? (Jaynes, 1976).

NECESSITY OF CONSCIOUSNESS?

We must conclude that consciousness is not necessary to the various perceptual phenomena—reactivity, motor skills, speaking, writing, listening, or reading. Is consciousness a state of experience? In fact, we must agree consciousness interferes with and inhibits what we have previously thought consciousness was. When attention becomes a conscious effort, the result is inattention. Is attention consciousness? Is it a synergistic state of affairs that integrates thought, insight, experience, and reactivity into one "form," of which only a "particular" has ever been seen? Is individual manifestation of a whole, one universe within a cosmos of consciousness, a holograph within a holograph, one fragment of the collective conscious? Is consciousness but an understanding imprinted upon the biocomputer in some electrochemical way that survives only as long as the organism? Is it but a concept itself that perishes upon death of the physical matrix? Is thought counterfeit, just a sort of mechanical, technological, biological, scientific matter?

Not many of us are inclined to accept the notion that consciousness is nothing more than a complex neurotransmission system that functions in many ways like a sophisticated computer, though perhaps deficient in much of its skill and reliability. Nor are we eager to view it as only a powerful energy field in the holographic metaphor without presupposing more—the implicate order.

What, then, is consciousness? To Jaynes, its manifestation is realization based upon language. As language evolved, so did consciousness, and vice versa, in a sort of chicken-and-egg relationship.

If our definition of consciousness is inadequate, how can we delimit its experience in neat little boxes that only exist dependent upon language constructs, which themselves are not necessary to consciousness? The seemingly infinite possibilities implied in "mind/brain stuff," not just of the human animal but of all species, does not yield limited necessary anything. Necessity implies contingency, for something either *is* or *is not* of necessity, which necessarily is perception relevant. Somehow "mind stuff" will not allow us to contain it in the organ brain or any other strictly finite function.

Then the question can be fairly asked, Is mind necessary to consciousness? And now we are right back in the thick of it, for are we speaking about conscious mind or subliminal mind? Or what do we mean when we say *mind*? Perception, like consciousness itself, not only is subject to our expectation set and our perceptual defense mechanisms but also is limited by the very nature of our definitions. In a sense, what we see is all there ever is, and all that *is*, is much more than what we see; and yet, somehow, we do indeed perceive what we do not see.

85

A fun, easy, and oversimplified example of but one of myriad mechanisms that function from limited and yet total awareness is offered here. Read it carefully and thoughtfully. Make certain that you understand the paragraph, and then put the book down and ponder its personal meaning to you. Then pick the book back up, turn to the following page, and follow the instructions.

FINISHED FILES ARE THE RE-
SULT OF YEARS OF SCIENTIF-
IC STUDY COMBINED WITH THE
EXPERIENCE OF MANY YEARS.
(Author unknown.)

Turn back to the previous page and count the *f*'s in the paragraph before going on.

_____

_____

_____

If you counted three, you are like most people. You pronounce *of* as *ov* and therefore probably missed counting the *f*'s in each of the three *of*'s that appear in the paragraph, and yet you know that you saw them.

CHAPTER NINE

A REVIEW OF SCIENTIFIC FINDINGS

*The principal ally of science is rea-
son. Reason is an artifact of experience. Science has often confounded
itself in the past, denying experience
in favor of reason.* —*Eldon Taylor*

SCIENCE AND SUBLIMINAL STIMULI

There has been much diversity in subliminal stimuli experimentation. Once researchers accepted the obviously implicit set that
accompanies varying levels of consciousness (aware to unaware),
studies proliferated and continue to do so, covering literally any
imaginable possibility. Evidence for the meaningful nature of the
perception without the awareness process (subliminal communications), specifically, the subliminal presentation of semantically
related or structured information, is what we will now examine.

It is exceedingly difficult to organize the array of scientific inquiries into the subliminal input effect other than chronologically,
which gives rise to redundancy. Therefore, I have organized the
information that follows in order of generally related categories. I
can highly recommend Dr. Dixon's works of 1971 and 1981 on

subliminal communication for a consistent development of the theory and implications thereof. Without duplicating Dixon's work, I have assembled a brief overview of data representing the scientific evidence of subliminal perception and some of its applications.

D. E. Somekh measured the effect of embedded words in a visual display. Content analysis of subsequent stories indicated significant correspondence between the presentation of emotive as opposed to neutral words. (Somekh, 1976.)

Support for the Poetzl phenomenon (the venting of subliminally perceived stimuli after the presentation of the stimuli—sometimes weeks later) was yielded from two experiments conducted at University College, London, England. Additionally, researchers concluded that stimuli presented in an unattended channel are fully analyzed for meaning and may be integrated with material in an attended channel when the stimuli are relevant to the ongoing task. (Henley, 1975.)

Graham Wagstaff, at the University of Newcastle-upon-Tyne, England, investigated the relationship between stimulus emotionality and perceptual sensitivity. Significant results support the perceptual defense hypothesis. Subjects were presented visual subliminal stimuli. (Wagstaff, 1974.)

A study conducted at the Psychiatric Research Center in Montreal, Canada, yielded findings suggesting that no difference in physiological response exists between the proven progressive relaxation technique and subliminal relaxation. (Borgeat, 1983.)

Fisher conducted multiple studies examining the mediating effects of subliminal auditory input upon the body boundary. In his findings, published in the *Journal of Nervous Mental Disorders*, Fisher concluded:

1. Significant and consistent differences between sexes exist in adaptation to subliminal messages of a diverse nature.
2. Interpretation of sex differences yield the theory that females are less threatened than males by the sensation that ''some force has gained entry'' to their interior.
3. Results support the hypothesis that, like all stimuli, subliminal input must compete with other information in its behavioral influence. (Fisher, 1976.)

VandenBoogert conducted a study of subliminal and hypnotic presentations based on a random sampling of audiocassette users employing self-appraisal methods. Subliminal programs consisted of identical dialogues to the hypnotic without the "count down" and "count up" verbiage. Results indicate a significant preference by users to hypnotic versus subliminal input by efficacy criteria. (VandenBoogert, 1984.)

Comparison of VandenBoogert's findings to those cited earlier at the Psychiatric Research Center in Montreal suggest that simple, emotionally rich statements are acted upon or accepted as more meaningful than hypnotic dialogues when presented subliminally.

Findings from a study conducted at the University of Rochester, where twenty phobic students looked into a blank tachistoscope while receiving occasional shocks indicate that expectancy plays a significant role in treatment. (Efran, Marcia, 1967.)

G. Smith, et al., of Lund University in Sweden experimented with a subliminal metacontrast design. Conclusions supported predictions. The studies were successful at manipulating identification with another person. (Smith, Gundmund, Carlsson, Danielsson, 1985.)

Roger Greenberg, et al., found evidence supporting Freud's penis-baby equation after demonstrating a link between phallic imagery and subliminal pregnancy messages. (Greenberg, Fisher, 1980.)

Donald Spence of Rutgers Medical School studied the effect of subliminal input on lexical decision time. Spence concluded that a priming effect was demonstrated for related primes where near-liminal related primes showed no such effect. (Spence, 1983.) Neurophysiologic data supports the effect of subliminal stimuli on decision making, demonstrating that unconsciously perceived stimuli has a determining role on the choice of reaction. (Kostandov, Arzumanov, Vazhnova, Reshchikova, Shostakovich, 1980.)

Helen Meyers of St. John's University studied the effects of a double bind introduced by conflicting auditory and visual subliminal input. Findings suggest that interactional patterns play a significant role in acceptance or rejection of double bind input. (Meyers, 1982.)

Henry Nicholson of Michigan State University examined the effect of contradictory subliminal and supraliminal (barely perceptible) stimuli upon viewers' perceptions of testimony presented on videotape. Findings suggest that jurors presented videotaped testimony can be influenced by supraliminal messages. (Nicholson, 1980.)

Poetzle's early work well documented the effect of subliminal stimuli on dream imagery. The Poetzle effect was discussed earlier. More recent research continues to demonstrate this effect. Gerald Murch, of Portland State College, did a study that yielded aftereffects of subliminal stimulation and interpreted the aftereffects as a function of the delay between stimuli presentation and reaction to it. (Murch, 1967.)

Shevrin and Fisher from the Menninger Foundation, derived findings supporting their hypothesis that changes in the effects of a waking subliminal stimulus are a function of the nondreaming and dreaming states. The presleep waking state, stage I sleep, and stage II sleep were distinguished in their evidence on the basis that the thought processes were found parallel to the psychoanalytic concept of primary- and secondary-process thinking. (1967.)

Strauch, et al., demonstrated that meaningful auditory subliminal stimulation affected sleeping behavior. (Strauch, et al., 1976.)

Dixon asserted that regardless of the paradigm in which unconscious perception is facilitated and despite the research context in which a paradigm is used, research indicates that there is a two-way communication between a sensory input, the human brain's unconscious memory system, and emotional evaluation and the interactions of sleep and dream states, microgenesis, and subliminal perception. (1983.)

Kaser also demonstrated effects of auditory subliminal messaging upon the production of images and dreams. Kaser sped the messages up and presented them by reducing the decibel level, while the messages remained loud enough to be heard clearly within a regular sized room. (1986.)

Jill Claire suggested a holographic model to the operation of dreams and demonstrated a link between the "seeds of past trauma" and disease. Claire asserted that in one of Freud's specimen dreams, subliminal physiological changes occur as a result of behaviors attributed to a complex when an image of disease is linked to a physiological complex. (1981.)

Donald Spence suggested that a stimulus may register outside of awareness and involve a change in perceptual sensitivity, which in turn then brings about an altered response (subliminal perception). (1967.)

91

Lee, Tyrer, and Horn used thirty-two agoraphobic patients to demonstrate marked improvement in the groups presented with subliminal messaging as opposed to the control or the supraliminal group. (1983.) Silverman studied supraliminal presentations and concluded that supraliminal presentations were not as effective (a view shared by other studies). (1971.)

Hebb proposed that incoming stimulation served an arousal function as well as an information function. (1955.) Testing this hypothesis with subliminal stimulation, Zenhausern, Ciaiola, and Pompo yielded findings that illusory experiences can be evoked and that the effect can be generalized. The greatest effect was achieved at 30 db below threshold. Further, their accessory stimulation design revealed evidence of a decrement in performance with the increase in illusory perception. (1973.)

Shevrin and Rennick found that subjects who exhibited the effect of stimulation subliminally had significantly lower B-wave amplitude of cortical-evoked potentials. (1967.)

Zwosta and Zenhausern tested the application of signal detection theory to subliminal and supraliminal accessory stimulation. They achieved their most pronounced results, measuring increased sensitivity, from signal strengths at -15 db (subliminal) to + 15 db (supraliminal), which represents the extreme levels incorporated in their study. (1969.)

Muriel Fox of New York University successfully verified the hypotheses that with regard to the basis of partially conscious cues, subliminal stimuli can be effective. (1966.)

David Somekh studied subliminal versus supraliminal effects with emotive and neutral words. His findings demonstrated the effect of emotive over neutral words but only in the subliminal condition. (1976.)

Silverman measured the effects of drive-related and neutral stimuli in subliminally presented material. He specifically observed their effects on symptomatology and ego functioning. Silverman's findings indicate that when subliminally registered, the drive-related stimuli will make contact with whatever congruent drive derivatives are active in the individual at that time. (1970.)

C. R. de Martino of New York University studied subliminal stimulation as a function of stimulus content. He presented drive arousal versus neutral stimuli. The words *kill* and *tell* were used. Results revealed that under neutral drive conditions, both stimuli were measurably effective; however, pre- to post-score changes, as reflected on the adjective check mood list, indicated that subjects who had been subliminally insulted felt more hostile and anxious. (1969.)

Gordon and Spence successfully demonstrated the sensitivity to a subliminal stimulus by arousing a congruent cognitive set in a drive-related stimulus. They used a subliminal food stimulus. (1966.)

The effects of subliminally presented aggressive stimulation on suicide patients yielded results demonstrating the relationship suggested in psychoanalytic theory between aggression and depression. (Rutstein, 1971.)

Another drive-related stimuli was studied at Sam Houston State University, in which subliminal sexual embedding in advertisements was the nature of the inquiry. Results suggested that sexual embeds influenced viewers, evaluations of advertisements. (Kilbourne, Painton, Ridley, 1985.)

Male homosexual psychodynamics have been examined involving subliminal presentations of either neutral control or incest-related stimulus. Results were interpreted suggesting that unconscious incest wishes stimulate homosexual reactions. (Kwawer, 1977; Silverman, Kwawer, Wolitzky, Coron, 1973; Kwawer, 1972; Mandel, 1970.)

Sexual and aggressive subliminal stimuli were studied by Antell and Goldberger in terms of their effect on creativity. Results showed that drive activation did facilitate creativity and that sexual activation was superior to aggressive activation. (Antell, Goldberger, 1978.)

At East Texas State University, McCormack and Jacob attempted to determine "if a subject's own admission of controlled attention was altered by varying levels of projected light intensities and durations of a sex-related subliminal message." The results proved their hypothesis. Subject's submission to a prescribed learning task increased with intensity and duration of sex-related visual subliminal input. (McCormack, 1980.)

That conditioning can take place on an unconscious, or subliminal, level was the conclusion of Beisgen and Gibby, who studied autonomic and verbal discrimination of a subliminally learned task at Virginia Commonwealth University. (Beisgen, Gibby, 1969.) Other conditioning studies clearly indicate that subliminal stimuli can affect attitudes and behavior. (Kostandov, Arzumanov, 1978;

Emrich, Heinemann, 1966; Hart, 1973; Genkina, Shostakovich, 1983; O'Grady, 1977; Soininen, Jarvilehto, 1983.) Subthreshold learning may also overtly interfere with subsequent task performance. (Brosgole, Contino, 1973.)

Direct measurements have been developed to examine and verify unconscious mental processes. They are approached from as diverse angles as frontal EMG, skin conductance, and heart rate. The studies and methods conclude that unconscious perception occurs, but repressiveness is a factor in the activation of brain and verbal responses. (Shevrin, Smith, Hoobler, 1970; Borgeat, Elie, Chaloult, Chabot, 1985; Gadlin, Fiss, 1967; Shevrin, Smith, Fritzler, 1969; Borgeat, Goulet, 1983; Watson, 1970; Shevrin, Smith, Fritzler, 1970; Libet, Alberts, Wright, 1967.)

Subliminal suggestions have been used during anesthesia to control postoperative complications. (Hess, 1981.) Subliminal perception and levels of activation studies indicate that visual and auditory subliminals influence the level of activation. (Borgeat, Chabot, Chaloult, 1981.) Visual evoked-response correlations of unconscious mental processing shows that encoded in the average evoked-response and influencing the content of free associations are the effects of subliminal perception. (Shevrin, Fritzler, 1968.) Changing the perception of behavioral properties through subliminal messaging was demonstrated by C. J. Overbeeke. (Overbeeke, 1986.) In studies of the effects of subliminal input on lexical decision tasks, perceptual defense mechanisms and the value of a priming effect have been demonstrated. (Spence, 1981; Williams, Evans, 1980.)

Models developed by Dixon, Fiss, Aurell, and others linking states of awareness, or consciousness, and personality variables with cognitive information processing have been only partial responses to accommodating the overwhelming evidence for unconscious perception. (Fiss, 1966; Aurell, 1979; Dixon, 1981).

The effects of subliminal aggressive stimulation on suicidal patients demonstrated that suicidal subjects showed significantly more depression following subliminal aggressive stimuli and a decrease in outward aggression and depression following the same stimuli presented supraliminally, as measured by the Multiple Effect Adjective Checklist. (Rutstein, Goldberger, 1973.)

Another comparison of subliminal versus supraliminal examined the effects of stress presentations on symptoms of anxiety.

Results showed that anxiety ratings were significantly increased where subliminal emotive presentations were involved and were reduced following neutral subliminal exposure. Additionally, in a comparison of supraliminal conditions and subliminal conditions, the correlations between psychic and somatic symptoms of anxiety were higher under supraliminal conditions. (Tyrer, Lewis, Lee, 1978.)

Subliminal and supraliminal presentations were made to three groups of five chronically agoraphobic patients. Both supraliminal and subliminal groups were found to improve significantly over the control groups. (Tyrer, Horn, Lee, 1978; Lee, Tyrer, 1980.)

Philip Sturman examined the subliminal arousal of unconscious dynamics of derivatives of the castration complex in normal adults. Three messages were presented:

1. Father castrates.
2. People walking.
3. Father argues.

Thirty-six subjects divided evenly by sex were rated for their castration anxiety both before and after subjection to the messaging. One of the findings indicated that messages 1 and 3 created psychic conflict at an unconscious level in normal subjects. This psychic conflict caused them to regress to earlier stages of development (regression hypothesis) with regard to levels of perceptual responding characteristics. (Sturman, 1980.)

James Robert Rudolph at the University of California demonstrated selectivity in subliminal perception relative to approach/avoidance tendencies. (Rudolph, 1970.)

The effect of subliminal aggressive stimulation upon young adults who had experienced the death of a parent during childhood yielded findings that demonstrated that subliminal aggressive versus control stimuli resulted in hypomanic defenses breaking down. (Miller, 1974.)

Harvey Lieberman at Pennsylvania State University presented subliminal stimuli through tachistoscopic exposure to study the relationship of developmentally determined personality and associated thought styles with conflict resolution. Results indicated that subliminal stimuli has influence over the direction of response without distortion of personality adaptation or defensive style modes of response. (Lieberman, 1975.)

95

A study design developed to examine aspects of the psychoanalytic theory of elation presented subliminal pictorial and verbal stimuli at New York University. Findings support the hypothesis that arousing aggressive drive derivatives may bring about depression. (Varga, 1974.)

The influence of subliminal analytic and introjective stimuli on normal young adults was a subject of study at the University of Southern Mississippi. Schmidt determined that on the basis of differing developmental origins, clinical manifestations, unconscious conflictual issues, and predisposing personality characteristics, there is a difference between an analytic type of depression and an introjective type of depression. This data provides some support for the psychoanalytic position proposed by Blatt. (Schmidt, 1981.)

Empirical verification of subception was demonstrated in a study designed to examine autonomic and verbal discrimination of a subliminally learned task. Seventeen subjects were presented ten nonsense syllables subliminally. The presentation was paired with a mild electric shock. Subjects were administered for discrimination tests. The study concluded that classical conditioning can occur at levels below conscious awareness. (Beisgen, Gibby, 1969.)

The effects of preconscious cues upon the automatic activation of self-esteem was examined by the Ledfords. Enhancement of self-esteem was shown in both mainstream and target experimental groups, and subjects identified as underachievers with socialization problems benefited slightly more from the techniques than did mainstream subjects. (Ledford, Ledford, 1985.)

Marianne Jeffmar studied ways of cognitive action. Examining the susceptibility to subliminal stimulation of the relationships of syncretism, flexibility, and exactness, Jeffmar's results show that combining syncretism with flexibility further enhances the susceptibility to subliminal stimulation and that this combination results in creativity. (Jeffmar, 1976.)

Using a metacontrast design to present subliminal stimuli in a study examining the relationship between creativity and aggression, findings suggest that creativity is higher in the self-reliant. (Smith, Gudmund, Carlsson, 1986.)

Evidence of unconscious semantic processing was the subject of one of J. A. Groeger's studies. Results revealed that semantic analysis predominated below the awareness threshold, while structural analysis of the target predominated below the recognition threshold. (Groeger, 1984.)

Visual subliminals were used to study the affective domain of learners. Of the stimuli content tested, sex stimulus was the most significant. (Ledford, 1978.)

Subliminal stimulus was shown to have an effect on associations of verbal content to the homograph, but not on latency, according to an article in the *Psychological Research Bulletin*. (Valind, Valind, 1968.)

A study conducted at the Polish Academy of Sciences yielded a clear effect linking semantical subthreshold stimuli with a shortening of the impulse transformation. (Czyzewska-Pacewicz, 1984.)

Five studies conducted by Dixon, Henley, and Weir examined the extraction of stimuli from continuously masked successive stimuli. The studies suggest that while the masked words are not consciously recognizable, they do not behave like totally subliminal verbal stimuli. (Dixon, Henley, Weir, 1984.)

The influence of subliminal perception on concept formation was investigated by Leclerc and Freibergs. Results indicated that only symbolic subliminal stimuli was effective in influencing the learning of a concept. The experimental design utilized metacontrast presentation, a process my research reveals is most effective with the right hemisphere, or the picture/symbol hemisphere, of the brain. (Leclerc, Freibergs, 1971.)

Smith, Gudmund, and Carlsson showed, using a metacontrast technique, that the main obstacles to creative functioning were rigid defense mechanisms and anxiety. Thirty-one psychiatric patients were presented a subliminal stimulus of a threatening motif as their experimental design. (Smith, Gudmund, Carlsson, 1986.)

Evidence of subliminal guessing ability was shown by the findings of a study conducted at St. John's College in India. (Singh, Devi, 1976.)

The effect of subliminal shock conditioning on recall was examined by Robert Harrison of Boston University. Results showed clear evidence for subliminal perception recall conditioning. (Harrison, 1970.)

Recall on word tests primed by a subliminal stimulus was the subject of a study conducted by Deanna Holtzman of Wayne State University. Findings suggested a significant interaction between the kind of words recalled with the subliminal stimulus. (Holtzman, 1975.)

According to a report by Keith Barenklau, subliminal technology is useful in technical training. Barenklau, in a journal paper, cited the use of a tachistoscope to effectively teach student drivers to recognize and respond to potentially hazardous driving situations. (Barenklau, 1981.)

A comparison of the aural arousal on the verbal learning of elementary pupils was conducted by R. L. Hylton. The effects of graduated levels of accessory auditory stimulation yielded the conclusion that subliminal arousal facilitated short-term memory. (Hylton, 1979.)

At Texas Tech, Robert Katz examined subliminal perception and the creative preconscious. His conclusion asserts that creativity was clearly enhanced by the preconscious incorporation of the subliminal stimuli presented. (Katz, 1965.)

It has been suggested in several studies that subliminal perception probably involves a different cognitive system than the ordinary. Numerous comparisons to similar underlying perceptual processes between subliminal perception and parapsychological phenomenon have been made. Most reports present correlates between the state of the individual and the strength of the signal. (Ehrenwald, 1975; Beloff, 1973; Dixon, 1979; Rao, Rao, 1982; Roney-Dougal, 1981.)

Hemispheric differences in information processing and subliminal susceptibility have also been examined by a number of researchers. The metacontrast design has been particularly effective where fear/threat stimuli has been presented. (Andersson, Fries, and Smith, 1970; Smith, Danielsson, 1979.) The influence of emotional subliminal content (words) on functional hemispheric asymmetry was the subject of one study conducted by Kostandov and Arzumanov. Their findings indicated increased diffusion over both hemispheres where emotional stimuli as compared to neutral stimuli was presented. Suggested by their work is a unilateral activation of the right hemisphere of the brain with a predominant role of this hemisphere in the cortical organization of the unconscious function with regard to unaccountable emotion. Also, unaccountable emotion was caused by the presence of a subliminal word which changed considerably the interhemispheric differences. (1986.)

Hemispheric asymmetry and selection accuracy of preconsciously acquired information and the processing thereof was investigated by Barchas and Perlaki. Their results suggest confirmation for the hypothesis that analytic subjects are more likely to engage the parietal region of their left hemisphere while holistic subjects were more likely to favor relative activation of the parietal region of the right hemisphere. Between parietal laterality and selection accuracy an inverse relation was discovered. (Barchas, Perlaki, 1986.)

Relationships between functional asymmetry, subliminal perception, and defense mechanisms show the right hemisphere to be superior, proportionally to the degree of hemisphericity in the preprocessing of emotionally loaded stimuli, although an interaction between hemisphericity and defensive style occurs. (Barkoczi, Sera, Komlosi, 1983; Cuperfain, Clarke, 1985; Mykel, Daves, 1979; Somekh, Wilding, 1973; Carroll, 1980; Foodman, 1976; Pajurkova-Flannery, 1979.) Additionally, verbal recognition is superior for the left hemisphere (normal forward speech as opposed to metacontrast) while visuospatial positional recognition is superior for the right. (Charman, 1979; Somekh, Wilding, 1973; Henley, 1976.)

The effect of gender, hemispheric preference, semanticity, and lateralization upon the sensitivity to subliminal auditory stimuli was studied at Marquette University. Results indicated that left hemisphere dominance increased susceptibility to subliminal stimuli. Subjects that processed data unilaterally as opposed to bilaterally were significantly more susceptible. (Hebeck, 1984.)

Sackeim, Packer, and Gur at Columbia University provided evidence supporting their hypothesis that the strength of subliminal effects is evidenced in individual differences in hemisphericity as well as in situational manipulations of cognitive sets. (Sackeim, Packer, Gur, 1977; Shifren, 1982.) Peter Walker demonstrated at Preston Polytechnic in England that despite the suppression due to hemisphericity (binocular rivalry), subliminal stimuli undergoes, as a currently nondominant stimulus, a full analysis. (Walker, 1975.)

At Lomonosov University in Moscow, USSR, perceived sound stimuli (PSS) and nonperceived sound stimuli (NSS) were compared for formation and development of temporary connections. Simultaneous elaboration of motor CRs to PSS and NSS were examined in humans. In the formation of temporary connections utilizing

99

the participation of PSS and NSS, a more pronounced EEG depression reaction was found with regard to the conditioned performance in the participating hemisphere. This was supported by the orienting response to NSS being significantly slower than the response to PSS using the development and extinction of electrographic components (GSR) and depression of background rhythmical activity. (Voronin, Novikov, Volkov, Dubynin, 1984.)

My own research in the presentation of audiosubliminal stimuli indicates a right brain preference for emotionally meaningful, authoritarian-style statements delivered in a metacontrast design while simultaneously presenting the left brain with comparably similar permissive statements, presumably entering without alarming certain defense mechanisms, delivered in normal speech patterns spoken slowly and meaningfully. In other words, the right hemisphere may be processing, from the perspective of primary hemispheric task orientation, "I feel good," delivered backwards (metacontrast); while the left hemisphere is analyzing permission to feel good via the statement, "It's okay to feel good." As discussed previously (see chapter 4), with regard to split hemispheric processing, the right brain function will perceive a word that is sung when it may not perceive a spoken word. Therefore, the statements appear to have greater effect when delivered in a sing-song, round-robin manner.

Nevertheless, one study conducted by Stefanie Glennon reported presenting pictures to the left hemisphere and words to the right. Significant results emerged by splitting the messages and congruent pictures among the group of subjects. The effect was carried by positive or oedipally sanctioning stimuli. (Glennon, 1984.)

One of the most outstanding contributors to subliminal research is Lloyd Silverman of New York University. Dr. Silverman developed what has been referred to as the oedipal fantasy, subliminal merging, oneness fantasy, symbiotic message, or simply psychodynamic activation. Without a doubt, Dr. Silverman and Dr. Dixon have pioneered the research into subliminal effects in this century within the western world. While Dixon worked on information-processing models, Silverman experimented with the symbiotic. It is not possible to examine current subliminal communication or subliminal information-processing theory without encountering their work. As Bohm and Pribram are to the holographic paradigm, Dixon and Silverman are to subliminal perception.

Silverman's symbiotic message consists of two statements:

It's okay to do better than Daddy

and

Mommy and I are one.

The mommy message is the most prevalent message studied. It is theorized that the mommy message appeals to an archetypical mommy imagery or symbol mechanism. It primes feelings of a perfect or mechanical mommy. It appeals to and in some ways satisfies frustrations or sublimination mechanisms produced by the oedipal principle. Derivations of the mommy message never work as well as the original. (Taylor, 1986.) Some have asserted that it is the oneness principle at work, and yet when "Daddy" and "Dad" are used, the result is disappointing by comparison. (Taylor, 1986.) My own research suggests that the power of the message is not in oedipal sanction but rather in the mechanical archetype mommy, or womb, from which rejection is unknown. Birthing itself is a rejection (ejection) from a oneness condition that nourishes, protects, and otherwise minimizes or eliminates the fear of rejection—a condition unknown while in the womb. This hypothesis is supported by other research. (Westerlundh, 1983.) (Remember our discussion in chapter 6 regarding real and synthetic fear and its basis in rejection, and see chapter 10 for a more detailed development of this line of thinking, together with some clinical findings from my study.)

Whatever the mechanism, the symbiotic fantasy has been employed to effect a variety of human experiences, attitudes, and emotions. It is noteworthy, however, that in order for the symbiotic message to have full efficacy, it must be presented subliminally. (Taylor, 1986.) Apparently, conscious attention to this message personalizes and thereby diminishes or rejects it entirely.

Susan Zuckerman combined "symbiotic gratification" with "sanctioned success gratification" to effect the academic performance of bright underachieving adolescents. Her results generally achieved significantly higher final examination grades for all experimental groups; however, the mommy message was found "to be conflictual for girls and adaptation enhancing among boys." (Zuckerman, 1981.) Supporting findings exist in Jackson's work. (Jackson, 1983.)

101

The effects of subliminal stimulation of symbiotic fantasies on the academic performance of emotionally handicapped students were reported in the *Journal of Counseling Psychology*. The experimental subjects showed improved adaptive functioning, and findings further suggested that an increase in the effectiveness of counseling and teaching can be facilitated through the activation of unconscious symbiotic fantasies. (Bryant-Tuckett, Silverman, 1984; Cook, 1985; Linehan, O'Toole, 1982.)

The effects of the symbiotic message on academic performance was evaluated in Israel using the Hebrew language. Results supported the hypothesis that the effect of the symbiotic fantasy with respect to the adaptation-enhancing effect represents a general human phenomenon. (Ariam, Siller, 1982.) Parker used the subliminal symbiotic stimulation procedure on sixty college students at the University of California at Los Angeles, deriving results consistent with those reported above. (Parker, 1982.)

J. Watson at Guy's Hospital Medical School in London, England, determined that Silverman's stimuli had different affective connotations generating different behavioral consequences through their efforts on the neural substrate of memory. (Watson, 1975.) This finding is supported by Pfanner's work. (Pfanner, 1983.)

Silverman found that the effectiveness of systematic desensitization resides largely in its activation of unconscious merging fantasies. (Silverman, Frank, Dachinger, 1974.) Emmelkamp and Straatman were unable to verify this hypothesis, however, through replication. (Emmelkamp, Straatman, 1976.) Silverman also concluded that unconscious conflict is temporarily resolved by the subliminal mommy message. (Silverman, 1975.) Silverman additionally demonstrated that the subliminal presentation of wish-related stimuli intensified psychopathology of various types. (Silverman, Bronstein, Mendelsohn, 1976.)

A study conducted by Sharon Hobbs indicates that subliminal stimulation of oedipal and symbiotic gratification may affect racial attitudes. (Hobbs, 1984.) Studies on schizophrenic psychopathology utilizing the symbiotic fantasy as an intervention have resulted in conflict reduction and overall enhancement of therapy. (Cohen, 1977; Silverman, 1976; Silverman, 1975; Mendelsohn, Silverman, 1982; Litwack, Wiedemann, Yager, 1979; Bronstein, 1983; Steinberg, 1975; Silbert, 1982; Fribourg, 1981; Kaplan, Thornton, Silverman, 1985.)

The subliminal symbiotic message has been shown to be effective in such applications as competitive performance, dart throwing ability, obesity, smoking cessation, depression, verbal time estimation, alcoholism, repression, death anxiety, stuttering, and asthma. (Sommer, 1986; Silverman, Martin, Ungaro, Mendelsohn, 1978; Schurtman, Palmatier, Martin, 1982; Dauber, 1984; Slipp, Nissenfeld, 1981; Burkham, 1982; Geisler, 1986; Feldman, 1979; Silverman, et al., 1972; Palumbo, Gillman, 1984; Silverman, Ross, Adler, Lustig, 1978; Brush, 1982; Palmatier, Bronstein, 1980.)

The purpose of this chapter has been in part simply to assemble some of the evidence for subliminal (unconscious) perception. This chapter represents a glossary of some of the more variant and significant examinations of subliminal perception and its application. Hundreds of additional references are available but have not been included.

As a criminologist trained in rules of evidence and procedure, I believe the case is overwhelming. As with evidence in any field, disparities are going to creep into the picture. Nevertheless, in light of the research evidence and considering the credibility of the researchers, in my opinion only a siloist would assert that preconscious perception is a fantasy with no hard facts behind it.

103

CHAPTER TEN

SOME CLINICAL OBSERVATIONS AND INSIGHTS INTO FUTURE APPLICATIONS

Service is the level of human activity where we take responsibility for any human condition which does not contribute to the growth, productivity, and well-being of those involved and we transform that condition into a context which produces workable solutions. —William A. Guillory

Clinical Observations

Studies by Progressive Awareness Research have been as diverse as the needs presented to us by prison systems, health care agencies, social service organizations, athletic teams, and individuals. Although most of what we will discuss in this chapter is clinical or anecdotal, it nevertheless yields some interesting information.

We have had the good fortune to work with, provide material to, and share findings with a large number of people—professionals and lay persons alike. For example, we conducted the first study of subliminal stimuli in an incarcerated environment. From this first study, a double blind conducted in 1986 (Taylor, 1986), the seeds for a continuing, successful voluntary program at the Utah State Prison was established. Files of pre- and post-test measurements (Thurstone Temperament Schedule) attest to the efficacy of the program. Many inmates have expressed their gratitude for this program, which they insist changed their lives. At the request of the affected inmates, and with their help, we created a "freedom from pedophilia" program. Success ratios were determined using pre- and post-plathysmographic measurement. The last time I was apprised, three inmates who used the subliminal program had post-test measurements indicating normal responses to slide presentations of adult females and children. (Mr. Lee Liston is the official who is owed a special debt of gratitude for making this program possible.)

One of the more interesting observations from this project came as a result of the affirmation lists provided us by subjects who were child abusers. Their lists incorporated statements which implied thought processes that were not previously identified in the thinking disorder profiles of pedophiliacs.

A free-standing adolescent psychiatric center in our area has employed different subliminal interventions on a number of occasions, and each time, statistically meaningful data was obtained.

The freedom from pedophilia program is but one of the programs developed in our research. We refer to these special programs as our "experimental-education" properties, and they include:

I Am Heterosexual
Bone Regeneration

Cancer Remission

Neurological Regeneration

These programs are available at no cost with a note from a competent attending health care professional stating that no contraindication to usage exists. We have assembled and maintained tracking files on the users. Some general statistics from our records yield findings based on self-reports (admittedly from small sample sizes) that indicate slightly more than 50 percent effectiveness. Given that there is no controlled application in these cases, the findings suggest a promising and exciting new specialty usage for subliminal intervention stimuli.

At this point two case studies are particularly relevant.

INTERVENTION

VW is a fourteen-year-old boy with a long history of physical disorders. He was born with vocal cord paralysis which affected his swallowing and digestion. This was corrected with a tracheotomy, and by two years of age he was functioning normally. Shortly after another child was born, VW began displaying symptoms of major illness. His illness was diagnosed as muscular dystrophy. By the time he had reached fourteen years of age, he was restricted to a wheelchair, with minor mobility to dress and bathe. In addition, he had developed a severe case of scoliosis (lateral curvature of the spine) and severe pulmonary problems. Attending physicians felt that the scoliosis was increasing pulmonary difficulties and that surgery, using fusion and metal bars to correct the curvature of the spine, was required. The attending physicians, while recognizing the value of the surgery, also felt that VW's pulmonary problems were such that he probably could not withstand the surgery—Catch-22, if you will.

VW's father came to Progressive Awareness Research to meet with members of the advisory board to discuss having a specialized program created for his son. After a review of VW's history, several factors emerged as significant. The first was that the severity of VW's illnesses and symptoms increased or decreased in proportion to the level of attention he was receiving. And second, VW was using illness to control his sphere of influence (family and friends). Third, there was intense sibling rivalry within the

106

family as a result of VW's illnesses. Fourth, parental inconsistencies and dissension had developed with regard to VW's treatment and care, which he manipulated to serve his purpose.

A special subliminal program was then created, using male, female, and child voices, recorded in round-robin fashion with full echo and reverb and using hemispheric processing. Affirmations were presented with authoritative and permissive dialogue targeting the following areas: self-esteem, self-responsibility, wholeness, wellness, the ability of the cells to replicate perfectly, acceptance, love, and specific messaging directed at the affected areas of VW's body. In addition, the forgiveness set and the mommy/daddy symbiotics were employed.

Because of VW's confinement to a limited area, different cassettes were created by mixing the affirmations with multiple primary carriers. One primary carrier selected was mixed ocean and nature sounds to allow him to study, watch TV, and conduct other activities using the tape as a noncompeting background sound. Other primary carriers selected were based upon VW's and other family members' personal preferences.

At the time these programs were created, VW had been removed from school and was receiving instruction in his home because of the complications of his illnesses. For a period of six weeks, VW listened to these tapes continually. At the end of this period, VW was administered pulmonary tests that yielded incredible improvement. The attending physicians were so encouraged by the test results that they felt VW was then strong enough to survive the spinal surgery. Within two weeks of the pulmonary tests, VW's mobility increased dramatically. His father sent to Progressive Awareness Research a picture of VW, previously confined to a wheelchair and his bed, walking up a flight of stairs.

After a few weeks VW began having problems with carbon dioxide retention. He was placed on an oxygen machine to facilitate his breathing. One evening his parents discovered that the oxygen had been turned up more than twice the prescribed rate. He was rushed to intensive care where he received treatment. While there his father noticed that VW's breathing pattern was similar to that of the period when he had had vocal cord paralysis. The physicians verified that VW did have the same paralysis, and a tracheotomy was performed.

At this time VW is experiencing a total recovery. His progress is being monitored, and updates are received as they occur. The physicians state that the only thing that can be said about VW's condition is that he has weak muscles. Is it possible that when subliminally confronted with the underpinnings to a maladaptive

108

defense mechanism, VW regressed to the point in his personal history of optimal health and attention?

CONTRAINDICATION

AC is a woman, age twenty-seven at the time of this writing, who began suffering from petit mal and grand mal seizures and blackouts at age twelve. Our objective was to create a subliminal program to eliminate these occurrences.

AC began having these problems shortly after the death of her sister. Her sister had developed complications from a cold, which produced breathing difficulties. AC tried to resuscitate her sister, without success, and her sister died in her arms. During the course of the next fifteen years, three additional family members passed away—two other sisters and a nephew. During this fifteen-year period, she had scores of blackouts and petit mal seizures, and she had five seizures classified as grand mal. Her blackouts would increase in frequency for a period and then remain dormant for short periods. The longest period of dormancy was twelve months.

After members of the Progressive Awareness Research board of advisors had discussions with AC and reviewed the information supplied by physicians, including recordings of a sodium amitol session, the conclusion was that these incidents were all emotionally induced and related to attention-seeking mechanisms. Of particular note was that certain significant people in her life, including her mother, had never witnessed any of these occurrences. Analysis disclosed areas of unresolved conflict in the following areas: low self-esteem, self-hatred, guilt, and religious conflict.

A subliminal program was created using male, female, and child voices recorded in round-robin fashion with echo and reverb. Hemispheric processing was used with both authoritative and permissive affirmations. Affirmations centered upon forgiveness, self-worth, self-esteem, freedom from guilt, and the reduction of stress.

Almost immediately after using the programs, the seizures and blackouts ceased. This continued for a period of two months before the blackouts and seizures began to reccur. AC's feeling was that she was getting close to a resolution and that her defense mechanisms were resisting her progress. She continued using the program over the next three weeks, during which time the occur-

109

rence of seizures became more frequent. During her blackouts she began behaving in a very self-destructive and suicidal manner. Some examples of this behavior included trying to exit moving vehicles and turning off the cold water in the shower, scalding herself.

In discussion with AC about these events, it came to light that she had stopped seeing her psychiatrist. For this reason, and because of the alarming frequency and intensity of these self-destructive blackouts, we insisted that she terminate use of the subliminal program.

Contraindications to subliminal intervention have been observed in other findings. Lorenzo's investigations contend that in certain instances subliminal stimuli may cause disorders of thinking and affective disorders. (Lorenzo Gonzales, 1985.)

William Bauer studied the effects of conditional and unconditional stimuli (subliminally presented symbiotics) on intrinsic motivation and concluded that description effects in styles of self- regulation could occur in subjects whose style was characterized by impersonal causality. (Bauer, 1986.)

As I pointed out in *Subliminal Communication*, legislative hearings have been unable to document an instance where subliminal intervention was dangerously harmful. I personally do not believe this is necessarily so any more than any substance or technology is free of the possibility of misuse, especially with certain pathological users. A segment of the population can and will abreact to almost everything. For this reason, it is my belief that subliminal manufacturers should use a "discontinue use" warning on their packaging.

There are both absolute and relative contraindications to the use of subliminal tapes. For example, the use of relaxation affirmations while driving vehicles or when operating dangerous machinery is absolutely contraindicated because of the likelihood of drowsiness. There are relative contraindications to the use of subliminals by those who have serious emotional or medical conditions requiring that they be closely monitored and supervised by an appropriate physician, because of the dramatic surfacing of underlying conflicts that occasionally happens. Such happenings may also be viewed as positive because they sometimes accelerate the discovery and treatment process that might otherwise take years to complete.

ETIOLOGY

One of the uncovering methods I have used in determining relative emotive content when scripting a subliminal audiocassette is the administration of a simple, self-designed adjective-relevant test with interpretation by means of psychological stress evaluation. The list of adjectives includes such words as *mother, father, love, hate, forgiveness, blame*. The Psychological Stress Evaluator (PSE) is an instrument developed by two military intelligence colonels and designed to test the veracity of a subject's statements without the necessity for physical attachments. Essentially the PSE measures the muscle microtremor activity that accompanies voluntary muscle movement, ordinarily at between 8 and 14 cps. The microtremor originates from the interaction between the sympathetic and parasympathetic divisions of the autonomic nervous system.

As I indicated earlier, all lie detection instrumentation is essentially elaborate biofeedback equipment. The PSE is an extremely sophisticated instrument that I used for years as a licensed lie detection examiner on criminal matters ranging from homicide to theft and in civil applications ranging from preemployment screening to executive personality profiling. The sensitivity of the instrument in subtle measurements of stress (as opposed to gross distress) makes it a valuable uncovering device. It is used for this purpose by many psychologists today. Many interesting findings have been yielded utilizing the PSE. For example, three statements that always produce stress are the forgiveness set. (See charts on following page.)

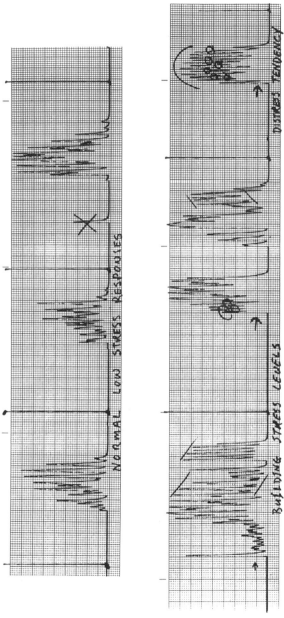

Examples are taken from a "no-jeopardy" demonstration examination (female subject   mode 3   15/16 IPS) utilizing yes or no responses to irrelevant, prestress, control, and relevant questions pertaining to self-esteem issues.

The Forgiveness Set

Every subliminal program we have created for the past several years has incorporated what I refer to as the forgiveness principle, or set. I am convinced that using only the forgiveness messages with the symbiotic messages would enhance every dynamic of human activity. The forgiveness set consists of three messages:

I forgive myself.

I forgive all others.

I am forgiven (in some instances: we are forgiven).

Earlier (chapter 6) when we reviewed the fear/anger loop, I suggested that the adaptive mechanisms were dependent upon blame and guilt for their function, and further, that their operation precludes the acceptance of self-responsibility, and, therefore personal growth. In other words, to the precise degree that we displace the responsibility for anything in our life, we eliminate the possibility to free ourselves from whatever limitations we experience. When we assume full responsibility, we empower ourselves for change.

All of my testing via the PSE and other measurements demonstrates the direct connection between fear/anger and blame/shame. By displacing this self-defeating loop, the displacement of problems ranging from self-esteem to self-inflicted poor health necessarily follows.

It is my belief that cellular learning replaces, or disorganizes, cellular memory. The result is disease. Paradoxically, disease is an outward manifestation of emotion which itself is generated through a lens normally dependent on false interpretations of the acceptance and rejection issue (drive, for that matter, since species and self-survival are dependent upon it), just as behavior is. Now, all behavior is behavior of choice, even if it is self-destructive (as is much avoidance behavior). In that sense, just as we choose behavior, we educate our cells to relearn (disorganize order). In a very real sense, we choose our dis-eases. What we create in our lives, therefore, is often what we fear most. What we resist, we become; what we dislike in others, we imprint on ourselves.

Interestingly, the adaptation process (avoidance of rejection orientation) also paradoxically could be said to operate from a law of the mind we could call defiance (the need for unique self-

113

expression). We could also say that the strategy of manipulation toward this end is the law of our psychology. Thus, the law of the mind is defiance, and the law of psychology is the strategy of manipulation, and chief among the victims of both is usually ourselves.

The value of a paradox to the philosopher is inherent in the circularity of its relative values. Thesis followed by antithesis provides insight into synthesis. The paradox of much of the human condition is that many of its preservation mechanisms work to extinguish rather than to preserve.

PLACEBO

When clinical observations or anecdotal information is presented, many people will immediately respond with placebo comparisons. The sugar pill effect is known to occur in approximately 20 percent of the population of any given study. The expectation factor (now known as the Pygmalion Effect instead of as the age-old self-fulfilling prophecy) predisposes outcome in about 40 percent of the cases. Neither of these statistical averages, however, accounts for the success of subliminal users. Our own self-appraisal survey correlated time of exposure (based on one-hour minimums per day) with measures of personally defined success and yielded the results depicted in the following graph:

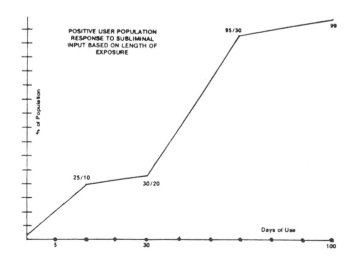

Still, the connection between mind and body is implicitly the ground of much that has to do with subliminal communication. In fact, to my way of thinking, it seems that perhaps ignorance has provided a fertile breeding ground for reasoning that traditionally has ignored the placebo effect. What really happens in the placebo effect is a change in organic chemistry and, to some extent, function (at least for the moment). The belief or expectation of the subject somehow reorganizes the body processes. It is not simply the mind cancelling a dysfunction that the mind believes the body suffers from.

Whether the cure is of a spiritual sense or arises from a placebo, one common denominator exists: the expectation of the subject is such that the cure is "known" to be imminent. What subliminal dialogues in general are all about is the production of positive self-expectations. Perhaps we should spend as much time studying the expectation phenomena as the pharmacological effects. Indirectly, and in some instances directly, that is what a large part of the study of neuropeptides is concerned with. Neuropeptides seem to serve as molecular messengers communicating with the immune system. It appears that emotions (expectations) and body function can no longer be distinguished in a precise and clear manner. A circular sort of communication system within the organ man has been described by neuropeptide researchers. (Pert, 1987; Wechsler, 1987.) It simply looks like this:

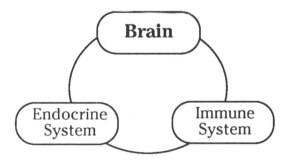

As we discussed in chapter 9, emotive responses are just one of the many areas affected by subliminal stimuli.

Now that chemical and neurological connections have been established between the brain and the health of the body (immune sys-

115

tem), perhaps the infamous placebo will become the famous sugar pill that patiently persisted despite its illegitimacy until science found a way to explain its power.

At the forefront of the neuropeptide research is Candace Pert. She and her husband, Michael Ruff, asserted that in essence every cell of the body has consciousness. (Ferguson, 1987.) Perhaps like our holographic information processing model or the holographic models of Pribram and Bohm, the body (from cells to total being) are similarly holographic or, in other words, simply smaller "parts" of the whole holograph, which is unfolding from an enfolded order and therefore is in "motion," as opposed to static, or holomovement. We will discuss the implications of this concept further in chapter 11.

FETAL LEARNING

Expectations are usually learned. Learning may begin earlier than many have formerly thought. Dr. Ron Conder of the Veterans Hospital in Cleveland, Ohio, has designed a fetal learning program that includes subliminal communication. Dr. Conder's theory is that mother and child equally can and do assimilate mental input "subliminally and subconsciously." The objectives of his program are to teach the principles of love, harmony, uniqueness, specialty, success, intelligence, beauty, health, happiness, social responsibility, and more. Dr. Conder believes that educating or preconditioning the child before birth will positively influence subsequent growth and development. I am personally very excited about his program, and we are doing everything we can to assist him in facilitating his product and experimental design.

Many individuals and institutions are implementing use of subliminals and studies on a continuing basis. We have provided cost free our technology and our experience to those conducting research. Within the near future, many of the questions still remaining about the subliminal learning process will be answered. It has been my pleasure to be involved in some of the unfolding of what promises to be a most powerful dynamic for the realization of human potential.

116

Audible and Subaudible

Earlier I discussed the neurophone and indicated that my observations yielded the opinion that it was more effective when used in tandem with hypnosis or an ordinary audiosubliminal cassette. This could be true because of the limited access the subject has to the neurophone, usually one forty-five minute session weekly.

Theorizing that the cognitive process could propel the realization of subliminal input, I designed audiocassettes that synchronized spoken affirmations with the identical subliminal affirmation delivered on the left channel (to the right hemisphere) and a permissive metacontrast adaptation delivered on the right channel (to the left hemisphere). Male, female, and child voices were used with full echo in the recording to obtain a singing effect on both the audible and the subliminal affirmations.

The programs are like a medicine—they may not taste good, but they work. One man I know had had little or no success with a variety of stop smoking programs. He used this "medicinal" approach (Positalk, I call it) and stopped smoking in two days. Months later he has no desire to smoke. He claims that listening to the program made his cigarettes taste nasty and his mouth feel dirty. He claims he either had to brush his teeth and wash his mouth after every cigarette or stop smoking.

Testimonies

My association with the Mind Mint stores (a franchise chain of self-improvement centers) has provided the opportunity to interact with hundreds of users of subliminal products. Recently, one of those consumers brought me an article in which two "prominent" authorities alleged that subliminal technology was a hoax. The user pointed out that the authorities quoted in the article had asserted that the only change a consumer of subliminal tapes would notice was a thinning of her wallet contents. This same user went on to relate how subliminal programs had stopped her child's bed-wetting and relieved her husband's migraine headaches. She purchased another four tapes.

The Mind Mint stores have sold literally hundreds of thousands of subliminal programs from many manufacturers, all with a money-back guarantee. Only a few dozen have ever been returned, and most of those were returned because of some defect in manufacturing. The subliminals industry sells millions of tapes annually and continues to grow. Chief among the reasons for their success is "word of mouth" advertising.

Now, this might all be anecdotal, but it is still statistically meaningful. No product survives, let alone thrives, in today's consumer market, if it does not work. Imagine selling an aspirin guaranteed to relieve headaches or a washing machine guaranteed to wash clothes that does not live up to its guarantee. Customers would quickly line up at the seller's door to return a worthless product.

Consumers are not as gullible as some so-called authorities would like to assume. History has many examples of the consumer market eventually pressuring the would-be authority until he reevaluates his position, only to discover that the consumer was right. In paraphrase, as Huxley once stated, the fact that a needle placed in the foot relieves a headache is a fact. No amount of arguing over how this is not possible will change the fact.

SUBLIMINALS IN SPORTS

My undergraduate alma mater, Weber State College, had not had a winning season in over ten years. When Coach Mike Price approached me about subliminal motivation stimuli, we designed a program that all of the athletes used. Using conditioned/response subliminal research, we decided to incorporate some key phrases that would be used repeatedly to "fire the guys up." The result found its way into national headlines when Weber went to the national championship playoffs.

Working from the Weber learning curve, several observations were made that are worthy of mention and that affected the present paradigm in use by three football teams—two college and one high school. First, we used a "come from behind" message, and in every game Weber played, Weber was behind at halftime. Second, we used "relaxed play" messages to minimize injury. (Weber went the season without a significant injury.) Third, the messages were all dovetailed to enhance team play as opposed to individual play. Weber had several WAC players of the week but no *one* superstar.

Improving individual and team performance in sporting events, using subliminal technology, has evolved into an area of research for Progressive Awareness Research because of the successful nature of the programs created for Weber State College. Since then, programs have been created and used in basketball, baseball, wrestling, and soccer, all with incredible results.

One of our advisers, a local soccer coach, used the program on selected soccer players. First the coach categorized the players into these areas:

1. Outstanding
2. Moderate
3. Poor

The team had two seasons, fall and spring. At the end of the fall season the coach rated the players and selected four players to listen to the program between the two seasons. Selection was based upon a mix of ability and parental consent.

Player	Overall	Team	Individual	Selected
1	2	3	2	
2	3	3	3	*
3	3	3	2	
4	2	2	2	
5	2	2	2	
6	3	3	3	
7	3	3	3	*
8	1	2	1	*
9	1	2	1	
10	2	2	2	*
11	2	2	2	
12	1	1	1	
13	2	3	2	
14	3	3	3	
15	3	3	3	
16	3	3	3	

The program used male, female, and child voices recorded in a round-robin fashion with echo and reverb. Hemispheric processing was used, and authoritarian and permissive languaging was employed. The affirmations were directed at self-esteem, confidence, speed, concentration, remaining calm under pressure, individual skills, teamwork performance, team skills, and positive expectations. The forgiveness set and mommy/daddy symbiotics were also employed.

Two weeks into the spring season, the coach evaluated team and individual performance. In addition, outside parties, unaware of who had used subliminals, were asked to evaluate player improvement and performance:

Player	Overall	Team	Individual
1	2	2	2
2	2	1	2
3	3	3	3
4	2	2	2
5	2	3	2
6	3	2	3
7	No longer on team		
8	1	1	1
9	1	2	1
10	1	1	2
11	2	2	2
12	1	1	1
13	2	2	2
14	3	3	3
15	3	3	3
16	3	3	3

With the four players who had used the program, a marked improvement was noticed, while the other players' performance remained about the same. The coach commented that the real difference between the players who had participated and those who hadn't was much more apparent than the ratings would indicate: "The players who participated had an increased confidence level, a willingness to perform, and a real love for the game. Their play with regard to other teammates was incredible. Soccer at times has a tendency to push for scoring and individual performance, minimizing team play. Without exception, the players using the program focused on team play, dramatically improving the teams' performance as well as their individual skill levels." Player 2 displayed a dramatic difference in play. In the fall he was timid and afraid to move to the ball; in the spring, not only was he moving

120

the ball but he was controlling the ball, passing to teammates, and even scoring goals.

One game before the end of the season, with a record of fourteen wins, one loss, and one tie, the coach ranked the players as follows:

Player	Overall	Team	Individual
1	1	1	2
2	1	1	2
3	2	2	3
4	1	1	2
5	2	2	1
6	2	2	2
7	No longer with team		
8	1	1	1
9	1	1	1
10	1	1	1
11	1	1	2
12	1	1	1
13	2	2	1
14	3	2	3
15	3	2	3
16	2	2	3

"The improvement of the team has been phenomenal," the coach commented. "I would like to say it was coaching, but I can't. The difference is the use of the program. The players using the program increased their performance and attitude. Their attitude was infectious and so was the ability to work as a team. I would like to use the program next year with all players participating from the outset."

The initial involvement with Weber and other successful athletic organizations led to the development of our present programs. Another season should reveal more data that will further fine-tune subliminal athletic motivation programs.

FREQUENCY ACTIVATION

One of our yet untested hypotheses suggests that various cellular groups within the body could be "sound" activated with subliminal stimuli. Just as there are critical and sympathetic resonant frequencies that control pests and herbs, there exist comparable frequencies that resonate to the body and particularly to sub- cellular groups in the body. A critical frequency destroys the organism, whereas a sympathetic frequency excites it.

A leading musician, Jim Oliver, has worked for years with Dr. Gorinda McRostie, measuring major and minor muscle groupings and their responses to wave frequency forms (sine wave, square wave, etc.), duration of intonation, notes, and so forth. These notes and wave frequency combinations and collisions have been proven to affect the physiology through testing using electronic measurements (such as EEG's). Their study of music with respect to psychological and physiological responses is known as "synphonics, or bioacoustics." This process has been used in conjunction with traditional medicine to promote health and wellness, specifically in cancer cases. Remission of the cancer has been the outcome in many instances.

Oliver, an Emmy Award-winning musician, can create notes over a range of ten octaves with a low side of 20 cycles per second and a high end of 20,000 cycles per second. Oliver and McRostie have identified specific resonate patterns that vibrate sympathetically to various regional cellular populations in the body. "We can focus right on a specific vertebra, and find the specific sound to adjust it," McRostie says. (Bartoo, 1988.) (See "Synphonics," this chapter.)

But now, imagine a cognitive skill like mathematics and the frustration of a predominantly right-hemisphere-oriented individual in his attempt to master math. Okay, now imagine a person listening to lectures on mathematics while in the background soothing music plays to disguise subliminal sound stimuli that activates, by its sympathetic frequency modulation, areas (cell groups) known to be highly involved in the learning and retention of left-hemisphere dominant skills.

Another scenario might be an encounter with the ineffable experience. Known areas in the brain, when stimulated electrically, will give rise to a deep religious experience. (See *The Biological Origins of Religious Experience*.)

Positron emission tomography (PET scans) have identified locational relationships in the brain with such things as hearing, seeing, thinking, and speaking. Further, PET scans have revealed specific areas in the brain that differentiate words from sounds.

Brain cell activity correlates demonstrate that regardless of the sense mechanism (seeing, hearing, speaking), words are processed differentially from other stimuli. For example, seeing a word excites (lights up, in the terminology of PET scan) cells in the visual cortex, which is at the rear of the brain, as does the sight of any image; however, where words are concerned, activity (lighting up) additionally occurs in the front of the brain (see diagram below). The study of the organization of the cortex has presented "hard" evidence that language information processing occurs along different (paralleling) pathways.

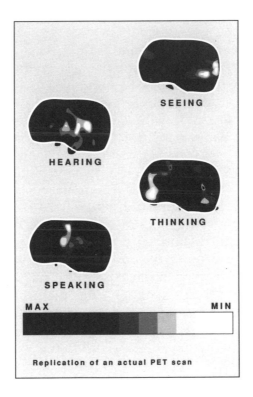

Replication of an actual PET scan

Until the PET scan, scientists often held that common pathways processed language in the same (although differing) signal (code) system as all other stimuli. Parallel processing not only allows the brain to do more things but to do them faster. (Kotulak, 1988.)

123

As the evidence amasses revealing not only processing means but the physical location within the organ brain for the phenomena consciousness, an entirely new implicit human technology is born, giving rise to possibilities that even science fiction writers have not yet explored.

There are many applications for this work. All that is needed is a few more years and several million dollars for research and development. Meanwhile, we will have to experience the ineffable on our own and continue to apply ourselves to learn.

Synphonics

One of the experts on sound and its influence on the body, Jim Oliver has used "synphonic" (body acoustics) music to facilitate the cure of many physiological dysfunctions. Oliver explains the process this way: "We experience sine waves as soft and gentle; this is a flutelike sound. Sawtooth waves are a trumpetlike sound. Square waves are like woodwinds. The human voice is a combination of all three types of waves. String instruments are square and sawtooth. In this work (referring to private sessions with synphonics), the client may respond to a second-octave from the bottom sine wave, and the response would be totally different if you played a second-octave from the bottom square wave." (Bartoo, 1988.) Additional research is continuing, and the findings will be made available in the near future in a book now being written by Oliver and McRostie. (It is worth noting that some subliminal programs are created using Oliver's synphonics as the primary carrier for the subliminal verbal content. See Taylor, 1986). Of particular interest is wave form (square, sine, etc.) together with frequency and nonstop antipestic rhythm as it affects different cellular groups in the body.

In a recent conversation with Jim, we discussed how sound waves could be used to control disease and rehabilitate atrophied cells. Jim has been successful at "vibrating" critical frequencies that destroyed certain invading organisms within the body. These vibrational frequencies are not always mellifluous to the listener. But as Jim puts it, if its pretty music that you are after, buy pretty music. Not all things are available in cherry flavoring.

124

We have incorporated body acoustics, including a number of Jim's compositions, in certain subliminal programs. Their efficacy is immediately apparent, although users sometimes initially resist the "music." Nevertheless, the mechanism of sound current is a promising and important aspect to be considered in subliminal mechanics.

DREAMS

I have been both student and teacher in a number of dream interpretation and cognitive dream workshops. The use of subliminal input to enhance dream recall and as a specific intervention for fear-laden repeating dreams has always been valuable. I have witnessed the integration of unresolved conflicts venting themselves in dreams in virtually every instance where appropriate subliminal stimuli has been employed.

Another observation is noteworthy. There have been many instances where an individual using a subliminal audiocassette in an autoreverse player during sleep has slowly awakened and, while in that threshold between alpha and beta brain activity, has clearly heard spoken the words that are normally subliminal to the conscious mind.

TOYS

It has been said that the difference between men and boys is the price of their toys. I often think of this statement when I look at some of my own toys. Among them is a Kirlian camera, which photographs the corona-discharge, or bioplasm, as it is sometimes called, of organisms. (This discharge is also called an aura.)

Soviet medicine uses the Kirlian camera (electrophotography) to diagnose and prognosticate disease. (Ostrander, Schroeder, 1980.) I have experimented with my own camera and subliminal stimuli and verified significant changes occurring in the bioplasma as a result. We know that by altering the mood of their thoughts people can affect this discharge. Many have theorized that it is an energy field that corresponds to that known as Chi energy, which courses about a meridian system in the body commonly identified with acupuncture/acupressure systems. Electrophotography illus-

125

trates seven major centers in the body that, interestingly enough, correspond with the Eastern Chakras.

Just by way of speculation, it appears to me at our present level of knowledge that this "third nervous system" is acted upon in a way similar to the other two, that is, by our perceptions of stimuli together with a servoloop of automatic processes (mind stuff), and that it affects the body. The difference may be that it could work as an early warning device. Since it is also affected or acted upon by similar subtle energies, like the energies of the environment, perhaps there is an exchange, or communication, that takes place subliminally at this level: bioplasm to bioplasm. If that reasoning is logical, then perhaps this third system is what we might refer to as holonomic; interpreting holomovement, or holographic packs of information, in a two-way process. All this is just speculation, mind you. But if it works this way, the additional "sense" that could be said to be holonomic possibly could be that mechanism that exchanges sensory input and that sometimes finds a path into consciousness or stores and transfers information that might come into consciousness. This could be a partial answer to the *how* of everything in the realm of psychic abilities.

TESTIMONIES

As mentioned earlier, I have heard hundreds of testimonies from users of subliminal programs regarding their efficacy. Most are in areas of weight loss, smoking cessation, and self-esteem. Because of their unique contribution to the inquiry at hand, a few are deserving of review:

1. My son is fifteen years old. He has cerebral palsy and very poor bowel and bladder control. We have tried every trick in the book to help him stop wetting his bed at night. I purchased one of your tapes, "Freedom from Bed-Wetting." My son has been dry for over two months now. We probably do not need the tape any more, but we still play it because it helps to put him to sleep. We love it, he loves it, and we are all proud of him for conquering this very difficult problem. —Virginia

2. I was legally blind before working with the vision tape. Now, with corrective lenses, I have 20/20 vision. —Mike

126

3. I have not been able to control my blood pressure even with medication. Since I used the blood pressure subliminal my blood pressure has lowered (145/78).—M.M.

4. My husband couldn't do anything at all for three weeks so we bought the creative intimacy tape. Within one week he was back to normal. Now he won't leave me alone—I'm going to hide the damn tape!—D.C.

5. I was in an automobile accident and suffered a massive hematoma behind my right eye. I lost consciousness at the scene of the accident and when I regained it, I had lost short-term memory skills. When nothing else worked, I used the neurological regeneration tape. After about thirty days of wearing my Walkman everywhere, I regained short-term memory abilities. My doctors were impressed. Thank you.— A.L.

6. Our family's experiences with the subliminal tapes have been very exciting and positive. Our son Adam, nine years old, has been tested and diagnosed as having ADD (Attention Deficit Disorder). We are presently treating him with the drug Ritalin, which acts as a calming aid to him. He has difficulties in controlling his behavior. We began having Adam, along with his brothers, read the affirmations on the tapes "Gifted Child" and "Neurological Regeneration," then we play the tapes at night while they sleep on an autoreverse, continual playing recorder through the intercom system into their rooms. Adam is now reading the affirmations morning and night on his own without being reminded. We are gradually cutting down the amount of his medication. His attitude is more positive, and he is really making an effort to control his behavior. We are looking forward to the time when he will be off medication and in control of his life. We feel the other children are more positive and cooperative, and each is improving in school. I personally feel more positive and calm and motivated in all my activities and in helping my family improve. I find the stress-free tape especially helpful in coping with the everyday life of a growing, active family. My husband, Jim, has made 180° turnaround in his life. He is a salesman by profession, and the "Powerful Salesperson" tape has increased his sales ability and sales to $200 to $300

more each pay period. He is motivated and always up emotionally. He says he actually feels a compelling force inside to do more. We are both setting goals personally and together, and it's exciting to watch our lives change to optimism and success.—Deanna

7. Deanna, age thirteen, had a bad case of acne. Within two weeks, there was a noticeable improvement, and within four weeks, her complexion was almost clear.—D.S.

8. I wanted to write to you and tell you what a difference the learning tape you sold me has made. When I bought the tape I was in the middle of midterms. I'm presently taking twenty credits at Brigham Young University, and the test load can be staggering. I listened to the tape for approximately four hours before I began to study and for nearly fifteen hours while I was studying. The results were impressive. I felt that I was able to accomplish more in a shorter amount of time than I had ever experienced before. I felt I was retaining more information and my mind was more clear, organized, and prepared for my midterms. Consequently, I was confident, and I did very well on tests. Thank you for your advice and expertise in choosing a tape for a skeptic.—L.S.

9. For many years we have had the responsibility of caring for my husband's aging mother. Since March 4th, it's been twenty-four-hours-a-day duty for various family members caring for her. A series of strokes has made it impossible to leave her alone. Through these difficult days and nights I have had special help. Prayers answered in my behalf, a caring family, and listening to all my tapes from the Mind Mint. "Optimism plus," "I am stress free"—the new weight- loss tape and many others have helped keep me calm and cool and collected during some very trying and exhausting days and nights. Without these added helps in my life, my eating disorders would be back in my life, dominating my stress-filled days. But even as my life turns upside down so to speak, I can be calm and serenity is mine.—L.U.

11. I was diagnosed with cancer and told there wasn't any help. I used the cancer remission tape, and when I last went for testing, the cancer was in remission.—J.

12. I taught a graduate chemistry course last quarter using the "Learning Is Fundamental" package. The average score

on the final examination was nearly ten points higher than that of the same class averages over the two prior years. —J.S.

13. I suffered from intractable back pain for years. No amount of medicine that I could use and still work relieved the pain. I used your pain-free subliminal in an autoreverse player all night long. The first night I tossed and turned and had several strange dreams, but when I got up the pain was gone. I use the tape every day and have not suffered the pain since. —A.

14. I had a drug and alcohol problem for years. Your people gave me the "Drug Free" tape. I no longer have a drug or alcohol problem, and I feel very good about myself.—L.

15. My son did not believe in subliminal tapes even though his brother has had great success. I played him the "I Have Clear Skin" tape every night at bedtime for seven days. He has had a skin rash for years that never disappeared. After seven days the rash was gone.—J.L.

16. My sister was in a coma in the hospital. I played your "Spiritual Healing" tape nonstop for two days. She not only regained consciousness but some of her first words were those from the subliminal script.—C.M.

17. My sister had a child born with only a brain stem. I obtained for her PAR's neurological regeneration tape. She played it in the infant's room. Within two weeks there was brain activity. The physicians, however, are not certain that the condition was properly diagnosed in the first place.—J.L.

18. I became pregnant with my first child late in life. Along with my doctors and family, I was quite concerned about complications with myself and my child. I used the "Miracle of Birth" tape set throughout my pregnancy. I delivered my son without complications or pain. It was a beautiful experience! Thank you so much for creating these programs.— V.M.

Subliminal stimuli has been proven to affect conscious perception, dreams, drives, emotions, memory, perceptual defenses, value norm anchor points, verbal behavior, and certain physiological functions or responses. (Taylor, 1986.) In the foreseeable future, subliminal learning (or relearning) techniques may become the

129

modality of preference to facilitate primary health care practices in the repair of dysfunctions of the mind and body. Perhaps, in the holographic sense, thinking is destiny. Whether placebo, pygmalion, medical anomaly, or miracle, one common denominator exists: the subject "expected" what occurred. Expectation is a creative force in the universe.

CHAPTER ELEVEN

A UNIFIED CONSCIOUSNESS PARADIGM

To give up everything known for nothing is to find the whole-thing; therefore:

EVERYTHING ÷ NO-THING = WHOLE-THING —Eldon Taylor

REVIEW

We have seen essentially two different paradigms for the failure to consciously perceive what we preconsciously (sub- or unconsciously) process. One form of subliminal communication gets in without conscious awareness because of our perceptual defense mechanisms; the other bypasses conscious recognition because of the technical concealment involved (tachistoscope, white sound, etc.). Implied in our understanding up to this point is the existence of data being perceived and processed without conscious attention in literally all units (packs) of information (stimuli) that one encounters.

131

Sometimes our inquiries become so detailed with minute specificity that we lose sight of the whole. Perhaps, in the metaphor of Alan Watts, we are without vision examining through a picket fence a cat as it passes. Many interesting parts give rise to generalizations about the behavior of the parts. Indeed, even cause-and-effect relationships can be observed, and if enough cats pass by, we may be able to infer with great accuracy events that will take place at the passing of the next cat. We might be able to say that a whisker appears before the eye and, therefore, the appearance of the eye is "caused" by the whisker.

THE WHOLE OF THE PARTS

Video games and home computers are an even better example of the point I wish to make. Let us assume that we are sitting in front of our computer screen with our joy sticks in hand preparing to shoot ducks that will fly over our boat floating in the water. Let's assume that the computer game has great graphics and the water swells and recedes, tipping and moving our boat just to increase the degree of difficulty in shooting the ducks. Further, let the ducks come in flocks sometimes and at other times alone. Now let's add some geese and recognize that we are penalized if we shoot a goose, even though they sometimes fly close to the ducks.

I hope you have our imaginary game clearly in mind now. It seems real enough as an out-there object or scene—unit of information, if you will. The more we play, the more our performance improves. We learn to lead the ducks and to anticipate the motion of the boat. Subtle differences are quickly absorbed, and we almost always recognize the geese, shooting only the ducks. Allowances are incorporated in our timing for the sensitivity of our joy stick. The monitor is alive with objects at rest and objects in motion. Logs drift down the channel that our boat occupies, necessitating moving our boat from time to time to avoid sinking. And now, imagine that you really have "gotten into" your computer game. If you would like, add a dog to retrieve your ducks.

The entire screen, although it seemed real in the sense that there were representations of parts (dog, boat, ducks) was no more than a mathematical program producing dots in series and sequence so

132

rapidly that what one sees is a boat or a duck. The dots mathematically progress, giving rise to the illusion of motion; whole things are moving and interacting through the joy stick as though they were indeed things in motion within a contained (total) environment. But they were only mathematical progressions programming dots.

Now the scientist comes along and says that there isn't a boat and there isn't really water. "The solid and liquid environment is really just a series of minute sequential dots, all of which are essentially the same."

Then along comes another scientist who argues with the first. Behind the dots is a mathematical program, an electromagnetic sequencing of the dots—you might say, a wave form.

So, first there were ducks and boats, then dots, and now wave form expressing itself mathematically. The more we separate the whole thing into parts, the less identity there is to it.

First it was a computer game, created to have fun, obtain skills, and experience. Implicitly, there must be a computer, an electrical source, and a programmer to write the program. And obviously there must be a player, or the whole thing would not occur in the first place.

The players interact with the game, creating their own sequence of events, which, without the necessary knowledge of the player, is interpreted by the game to create the next set of sequences in accordance with the invisible matrix of the software. The dynamics of the total (whole) interaction (implicate and explicate set) are much more than of *a* dot, or several dots, or the mathematical schema, or any of the parts.

Now, assume that we are, metaphorically, all programmers and players in a world that is the game. We are not outside of the terminal but rather inside (within) the screen. Earlier we accepted a role within the screen when we shot the ducks. Our primary *us* was nevertheless outside of the screen—we were just pretending to be in the screen. In life, however, we are primarily inside extrapolating outward. From within we imagine the "without."

Perhaps from within it becomes easier to grasp that all information on the screen is relevant to us but not really apart from us. The information (program sequence) is codependently interactive.

From within or without, we are both the player and the playee—both the hand on the gun in the boat and the hand on the joy stick. Whatever we do becomes a part of the total information set for the next sequence. The event and the participator are co-dependent variables interacting in a larger information set producing unique outcomes from a general systems program.

Mathematics is one such general system program, or at least an observation point providing insight to the program. Math is essentially a proposition of equality. That is, a mathematical statement is a formula for verifiable information sets. We all learn to check our math by reversing the process. Multiply 4 by 2, and the answer will be divisible by 2 and equal 4. So we multiply and check our multiplication by division, and we divide and check our division by multiplication, and we do the same thing with addition and subtraction.

We see that the logic of math is somewhat the logic of our understanding of ourselves and the universe. Quantifiable this and that is what separates hard science from theology, physics from metaphysics. Pythagoras used mathematics to make observations that revealed the systematic sequence of order and creation (teleology). The relation of man to the universe and ultimately to God could be approached by understanding the logic of creation.

The zero in mathematics is nothing and everything. Ten to the tenth power is an expression of the exponential power of zero. Zero added to or subtracted from a number does not change the number. Multiply by zero and the answer is always zero. Division by zero results in the same logic that division of the whole reveals—a logic that implies more than the parts undergoing division (as was the instance with Watt's cat analogy or my computer game analogy). In fact, the closer we get to zero in division, the more of the whole becomes implicate, or necessarily implicit. A simple example follows:

$$8 \div 8 = 1$$
$$8 \div 4 = 2$$
$$8 \div 2 = 4$$
$$8 \div 1 = 8$$
$$8 \div 1/2 = 16$$
$$8 \div 1/4 = 32$$
$$8 \div 1/8 = 64$$
$$8 \div 1/16 = 128$$
$$8 \div 1/32 = 256$$
$$8 \div 0 = \infty \text{ (undefined)}$$

134

Whole Stimuli

Information comes in sets or packs. It is the whole of the stimuli—not some linearly conscious part. The whole of the universe represents itself in whole units as do the cells of the body or the functions of the brain. Is this a codependent variable general-systems wholeness? Absolutely! And it has been termed the holographic paradigm. Karl Pribram, a neuroscientist, and David Bohm, a physicist, put the theory this way, according to Marilyn Ferguson of the *Brain/Mind Bulletin*:

> Our brains mathematically construct "concrete" reality by interpreting frequencies from another dimension, a realm of meaningful, patterned primary reality that transcends time and space. The brain is a hologram, interpreting a holographic universe. (Wilbur, 1982.)

In Bohm's terminology, there exists an implicate realm of wholeness, orderly and unified, beneath the explicate realm of separateness (things and events). Bohm refers to this description or reality as the enfolded order. He asserts that classical reality has been observed in a self-defined (piece and part) unfolded order. Primary reality is a frequency realm—an invisible matrix. (Ibid.)

Karl Pribram has assembled evidence over the past fifteen plus years to show that the "deep structure" of the brain is principally holographic. Pribram is convinced that the brain constructs mental properties by organizing the data input through the senses from the physical world and, paradoxically, that these same mental properties are the principle behind organizing the physical world, including the brain. (Ibid.)

Dennis Gabor mathematically demonstrated and named the hologram in the late 1940s. His equations demonstrated the paradox inherent to the hologram, chiefly that the same "mathematical transfer function transformed object into wave storage and move storage into image! The storage of wave patterns is thus reciprocally related to the imaging of objects!" (Ibid.) (See chapter 2.)

Karl Pribram, in *The Holographic Paradigm and Other Paradoxes*, explains the holographic brain this way:

> Essentially, the theory reads that the brain at on stage of processing performs its analyses in the frequency domain. This is accom-

135

plished at the junctions between neurons, not within neurons. Thus graded local waxings and wanings of neural potentials (waves) rather than nerve impulses are responsible. Nerve impulses are generated within neurons and are used to propagate the signals that constitute information over long distances via long nerve fibers. Graded local potential changes, waves, are constituted at the ends of these nerve fibers where they adjoin shorter branches that form a feltwork of interconnections among neurons. Some neurons, now called local circuit neurons, have no long fibers and display no nerve impulses. They function in the graded wave mode primarily and are especially responsible for horizontal connectivities in sheets of neural tissue, connectivities in which holographic-like interference patterns can become constructed. (Ibid.)

If the world of shoes and ships and sealing wax is essentially holographic wave form and the brain is recording these interference patterns (mathematical expressions of wave form) holographically, it follows that the mechanism for information processing is a holographic interface, or lens, if you will.

Examining the proposed model from chapter 2, we can observe the same circularity that exists in the paradox of the entire paradigm. The entire perception/manifestation process is codependent.

The entire process, like the dots on the computer screen, is reducible to mathematically ordered wave form, which generates dimensional explicate form from a formless implicate order, but there is more than one player. Each of us has, or more functionally *is*, a terminal accessing the same main frame.

The whole of the data available in a holograph exists in each of its parts, regardless of how many pieces you cut from it. The smaller the piece, the less resolute the detail; nevertheless, the whole is still represented in each part.

Each of us is interacting (existing) as *a* piece in the whole and therefore representative *of* the whole. In that sense, and to that precise degree, much more information is available to each of us than the normal conscious lens even ascertains. The collective unconscious of Jung is perhaps but a level of consciousness in a collective whole or a unified consciousness, additive and immutable. It is my opinion, as set forth fully in my book *Exclusively Fabricated Illusions*, that consciousness participates within itself, that thought can be viewed as an electromagnetic wave form, and the organ (homo-sapien sapien—cells, senses, brain, etc.) is a transceiver. Mind stuff is, therefore, interconnected with other mind stuff, as physical this is with physical that, and as they both are with each other.

Subliminally, we process packs of information simultaneously. Each of these packs is holographic. All information is encoded in the brain and meaningful information is imprinted upon the body. A traumatic experience (event interpretation) gives rise to the need to punish oneself (a fear based blame/shame reaction) and the result is an illness. One year later, the trauma may be mostly outgrown, yet there is sudden illness again. All of the sensory input surrounding the trauma is imprinted on the body, which recognizes some of that input, perhaps including the season or time of year, and "remembers" to produce the illness as a learned coping procedure. It is from this etiological perspective of dysfunction, together with that discussed earlier as the rejection/fear loop and the forgiveness principle, that my subliminal stimuli designs have been generated. (See chapters 5, 6, and 10.)

The strings of the holographic universe are the results of the actions and interactions of infinitesimal waves that act and are acted upon as the waves interfering with each other when two identical pebbles are dropped into a pond. As Bohm points out, "any form of movement could constitute a hologram, movements known or unknown and we will consider an undefined totality of movement, called the holomovement and say: the holomovement is the ground of what is manifest." (Ibid.)

The conscious mind of the individual, as Libet has put it, simply selects from among possibilities developed by the unconscious. (Bower, 1986.)

Professor William Guillory and I chatted one evening about subliminal perception, this work, some of my "models" for understanding, and the current trend in "hard science." The next morning, he stopped by my office with this:

> The basic nature of the Universe is energy in an infinite array of vibrational frequencies, manifested in an infinite variety of forms. These forms serve as a means of consciousness evolution. Everything (entity) that exists, vibrates within this spectrum of coalesced or uncoalesced form, as limited by the human senses. Any material

137

form which is manifested is simply a converted form of energy having some frequency of oscillation (vibrational frequency). The source of this vibrational frequency is inherent in the dynamic nature of energy (light) itself. Every rock, plant, animal human form, atom is a chosen experiment created by the Flow, the tendency toward consciousness evolution.

The "New Scientific Paradigm" will no longer assume theories and laws to have anything to do with reality. It acknowledges the attempt to describe reality as illusion. Therefore, the new paradigm of science will be to harmoniously use the illusionary objective world to understand ourselves. In other words, physics and every other discipline in its own unique fashion is the study of consciousness.

The "New Consciousness" will shift the role of the planet's philosophies (not political) and religions to realize their oneness of intention; and that being realization of absolute oneness of every entity in the cosmos, the Spiritual consciousness. To view their basic role as assisting each individual to take personal responsibility to "look" within themselves.

The major difference in procedure between the Spiritual and the Scientific is acceptance in learning without and with proof of consistency of acquired knowledge (not wisdom), respectively.

CONCLUSION

Dixon prefaced his information-processing model as one which was necessary in order to avoid metaphysical interpretation of the nomenon and phenomenon that accompanies consciousness. I take no such stand, and I offer no apology for it. Accepting, at least as an alternative, the unified consciousness paradigm, is admitting metaphysical conclusions. In my opinion, this is the direction, or shall I say redirection, of science today.

Behavioral science is no exception. Transformational psychology is just another title for pastoral psychology. As a pastoral psychologist myself, I welcome behaviorists as well as cognitive and humanistic psychologists to the spiritual experience. Albert Einstein said it well:

> While it is true that scientific results are entirely independent from religious or moral considerations, those individuals to whom

we owe the great creative achievements of science were all of them imbued with the truly religious conviction that this universe of ours is something perfect and susceptible to the rational striving for knowledge. (1964.)

CHAPTER TWELVE

ONE LAST THOUGHT

I want to know God's thoughts
. . . the rest are details.
—Albert Einstein

As Bohm and Peat more than adequately show in *Science, Order and Creativity,* the evolution of man's awareness of himself and the means by which he manipulates his universe (science) is better served when differences are examined as additive rather than opposing. In an exclusive and additive way, I have sometimes presented ostensibly opposing views, attempting to incorporate models and mechanisms that facilitate each other in nonmutually exclusive ways.

To the discerning reader, this will be obvious. To those entrenched in the *only* right way, this will be difficult. No matter, for discursive intellect is after all bound within its inherent polarity and thus the dialectic method. To me, science is as Max Planck once said: it "means unresting endeavour and continually progressing development toward an aim which the poetic intuition may apprehend, but which the intellect can never fully grasp." (Lukav, 1980.)

Thank you for your time, and may all that you may become be yours!

SUPPLIERS
OF SUBLIMINALS

Accelerated Learning Institute
P.O. Box 8276
Silver Spring, MD 20910

Advanced Learning Systems,
Inc.
7131 Owensmouth Ave.
Canoga Park, CA 91303

Adventures in Learning
1260 Hornby St.
Vancouver, BC V621W2

Alphasonics International
P.O. Box 3333
Stuart, FL 34995

Audio Activation, Inc.
Waterside Plaza, Suite 14A
New York, NY 10010

Earth Education
P.O. Box 747
Fairfield, IA 52556

Effective Learning Systems,
Inc.
5221 Edina Ind. Blvd.
Edina, MN 55435

Escott International
3275 Mautin Rd.
Walled Lake, MI 48088

Futurehealth, Inc.
975 A Bristol Pike
Bensalem, PA 19020

Gateways Research Institute
P.O. Box 411
Ojai, CA 93023

Steven Halpern
260 W. Broadway
New York, NY 10013

Hypnovision Video
25 Dryden Lanee
Providence, RI 02904

Image Dynamics
557 California Street
Suite 118
Boulder City, NM 89005

John-David Learning Institute
2740 Roosevelt St.
Carlsbad, CA 92008

Llewellyn Publishing
Box 64383-88B
St. Paul, MN 55164

Light Unlimited
HC02 Box 943
Cave Creek, AZ 85331

Mankind Research Unlimited,
  Inc.
1315 Apple Ave.
Silver Spring, MD 20910

Metacom
1401–B West
River Road N
Minneapolis, MN 55411

Midwest Research
6515 Highland Rd. #203
Pontiac, MI 48054

Mind Mint
4150 So. 1785 W.
Salt Lake City, UT 84119

Mind Communications
945 Burton SW
Grand Rapids, MI 49509

Mystic Trader
Box 24966
Coeur d'Alene, ID 83814

Nightingale-Conant Corp.
7300 North Lehigh Ave.
Chicago, IL 60648

Oliver Music
Jim Oliver
P.O. Box 6508
Santa Fe, NM 87502

Potentials Unlimited
4808 Broadmore
Grand Rapids, MI 49508

Power Learning
22704 Ventura Blvd..
Woodland Hills, CA 91364

Progressive Awareness
  Research, Inc.
Box 73617
Salt Lake City, UT 84107

Psychodynamics
3202 W. Anderson Lane #203
Austin, TX 78757

Reflections
Box 1249
Carmel Valley, CA 93924

Mary Richards
881 Hawthorne Dr.
Walnut Creek, CA 94596

Louis Shirley, M.D.
Shirley Tapes
Jennings, LA

Success Education Institute
Box 9068
San Diego, CA 92109–3602

Success World
83 King Street, Suite 220
Seattle, WA 98104

Superlearning
450 Seventh Ave.
New York, NY 10123

Threshold Research Assoc.
22704 Ventura Blvd.
Woodland Hills, CA 91364

Valley of the Sun
Box 2010
Malibu, CA 90265

Warner Audio
Box 211
New York, NY 10011

Western Research Institute
P.O. Box 7443
Thousand Oaks, CA 91359

RECOMMENDED READINGS

Adams, V. May 1982. "Mommy and I are one": Beaming messages to inner space. *Psychology Today,* 16 (9),24.

Adamson, R.; Henke, P.; and O'Donovan, D. 1969. Avoidance conditioning following preadaptation to weak shock. *Psychonomic Science,* 14 (3), 119–21.

Advertising Age. 11 Feb. 1985, pp. 2, 84. Dingell dangles clout over alcohol hearings.

Advertising Age. 5 Jan. 1981, p. 36. Inappropriate modifiers can seriously water down an ad message, warns Social Research, Inc. Chicago: BB Gardner.

Advertising Age. 13 Aug. 1984, p. 6. Spirits industry beams over BATF review.

American Metal Market. 16 Aug. 1984, p. 14. Shoplifting reduced 80 percent by subliminal technology.

Anonymous. July 1986. Subliminal messages: Subtle crime stoppers. *Chain Store Age Executive,* 62 (7), 85, 88.

Antell, M. J. Feb. 1970. The effect of priming and the subliminal presentation of sexual and aggressive stimuli on tests of creativity. *Dissertation Abstracts International,* 30 (8–B), 3859–60.

Ariam, S. May 1980. The effects of subliminal symbiotic stimuli in Hebrew on academic performance of Israeli high school students. *Dissertation Abstracts International,* 40 (11–1), 5782.

Ariam, S., and Siller, J. 1982. Effects of subliminal oneness stimuli in Hebrew on academic performance of Israeli high school students: Further evidence on the adaptation-enhancing effects of symbiotic fantasies in another culture using another language. *Journal of Abnormal Psychology,* 91 (5).

Arzumanov, IuL. Sept.-Oct. 1974. Elaboration of temporary connections in man using unrecognized visual stimuli. *Zb Vyssh Nerv Deiat,* 24 (5), 917–23.

Augenbraun, H. R. June 1983. The effect of subliminal activation of unconscious fantasies in the treatment of juvenile-onset and adult-onset obesity. *Dissertation Abstracts International,* 43 (12–B), 4134.

Babighian, G. July-Aug. 1969. Behavior and clinical importance of various subliminal tests in Menier's disease. *Minerva Otorinolaringo* (Italy), 19 (4), 215–22.

Bagby, P. K. June 1985. The effect of symbiotic and oedipal subliminal stimuli on field independence and competitive tasks. *Dissertation Abstracts International,* 45 (12–B, Ft 1), 3927.

Baker, L. E. 1937. The influence of subliminal stimuli upon verbal behavior. *Journal of Experimental Psychology,* 20.

Balota, D. A. June 1982. Automatic and attention activation in semantic and episodic memory: Implications for the utility of conscious awareness. *Dissertation Abstracts International,* 42 (12–B,Pt 1), 4952.

Bancroft, W. J. 1976. Suggestology and suggestopedia: The theory of the Lazonov method.

Banreti-Fuchs, K. M. 1967. Perception without awareness. *Acta Psychologia* (Amsterdam, Netherlands), 26 (2), 148–60.

Barber, P. J. Aug. 1977. Experimenter bias against subliminal perception? A rejoinder. *British Journal of Psychology,* 68 (3), 281–82.

Barber, P. J., and Rushton, J. F. Aug. 1975. Experimenter bias and subliminal perception. *British Journal of Psychology,* 66 (3), 357–72.

Bargh, J. A.; Bond, R. N.; Lombardi, W. J.; and Tota, M. E. May 1986. The additive nature of chronic and temporary sources of construct accessibility. *Journal of Personality and Social Psychology,* 50 (5), 869–78.

Battersby, W. S., and Defabaugh, G. L. July 1969. Neural limitations of visual excitability: After-effects of subliminal stimulation. *Vision Research* (England), 9 (7), 757–68.

Bayuk, M., and Bayuk, S., comps., 1980. *Suggestology and Suggestopedia: A Selective Bibliography of Western Sources.*

Becker, H. C.; Chamberlain S.; Burt, S.; Heisse, J.; and Marino, D. Poster session reported to the American Society of Clinical Hypnosis, 25th Annual Scientific Meeting.

Becker, H. C., and Charbonnet, K. D. 28 Mar. 1980. Applications of subliminal video and audio stimuli in therapeutic, educational, industrial, and commercial settings. Eighth Annual Northeast Bioengineering Conference, Massachusetts Institute of Technology, Cambridge.

Becker, H. C.; Corrigan, R. E.; Elder, S. T.; Tallant, J. D.; and Goldstein, M. 22–27 Aug. 1965. Subliminal communication: biological engineering considerations. In *Digest of the 6th International Conference on Medical Electronics and Biological Engineering,* pp. 452–53. Tokyo, Japan.

Becker, H. D., and Elder, S. T. 5–11 Sept. 1966. Can subliminal perception be useful to the psychiatrist? *Excerpta Medica* (International Congress Series No. 117). Abstract of paper presented to the IV World Congress of Psychiatry, Madrid, Spain.

Becker, H. C., and Glauzer, N. H. 10–12 Apr. 1978. Subliminal communication: Advances in audiovisual engineering applications for behavior therapy and education. *Proceedings of the 1978 Institute of Electrical and Electronics Engineering* Region 3 Conference.

Becker, H. C.; Jewell, J. F.; and Alito, P. 13–17 Mar. 1977. Video and audio signal monitors/processors for subliminal communication in weight control. *Proceedings of the 112th Annual Meeting of the Association for the Advancement of Medical Instrumentation* (AAMI). San Francisco.

Becker, H. C., and McDonagh, E. W. Nov. 1979. Subliminal communication (subliminal psychodynamic activation) in rehabilitative and preventive medicine. *Proceedings of the Ninth Annual Conference of the Society for Computer Medicine.* Atlanta.

Bell, P. D. Apr. 1986. The interspersal technique of Milton Erickson: Testing an operational definition. *Dissertation Abstracts International,* 46 (10–B), 3586–87).

Ben-Hur, A. Nov. 1970. The relationship of systematic desensitization and the activation of symbiotic merging fantasy to speech anxiety reduction among college students. *Dissertation Abstracts International,* 40 (5– B), 2351–52.

147

Bender, B. G. Dec. 1973. Spatial interactions between the red- and green-sensitive colour mechanisms of the human visual system. *Vision Research,* 13 (12), 2205–18.

Bernstein, B. R. Feb. 1986. The effects of subliminal symbiotic and oedipal stimuli on weight loss in obese women. *Dissertation Abstracts International,* 46 (8–B), 2795.

Berry, D. M. May 1985. Effects of educative/support groups and subliminal psychodynamic activation on bulimia in college women. *Dissertation Abstracts International,* 45 (11–B), 3612.

Bevin, W. Feb. 1964. Subliminal stimulation: A pervasive problem for psychology. *Psychological Bulletin,* 61 (2), 84–92.

Blum, G. S. Dec. 1975. Reply to Jennings and George. *Perceptual and Motor Skills,* 41 (3), 957–58.

Bouchard, S. J. Dec. 1984. Effects of a self-administered subliminal relaxation treatment on anxiety. *Dissertation Abstracts International,* 45 (6–B), 1906.

Bower, B. 8 Mar. 1978. Subliminal messages: Changes for the better? *Science News,* 129 (3), 156.

Brandeis, D., and Lehmann, D. 1986. Event-related potentials of the brain and cognitive processes: Approaches and applications. *Neuropsychologia,* 24 (1), 151–68.

Brennan, S. M. Dec. 1984. The effect of subliminal separation-individuation schemas on moral reasoning and mood in depressed and nondepressed women. *Dissertation Abstracts International,* 45 (6–B), 1907.

Bromfield, R. N. May 1986. Subliminal psychodynamic activation: Demonstration, oedipal factors and personality correlates. *Dissertation Abstracts International,* 46 (11–B), 4005.

Bryant-Tuckett, R. M. June 1981. The effects of subliminal merging stimuli on the academic performance of emotionally handicapped students. *Dissertation Abstracts International,* 41 (12–B), 4654.

Budzynski, T. 1977. Tuning in on the twilight zone. *Psychology Today,* 11 (3), 38–44.

Carter, R. Jan.-Feb. 1986. Whispering soft nothings to the shop thief: How 'reinforcement messaging' works. *Retail and Distribution Management* (UK), 14 (1), 36, 39.

Chain Store Age Executive Edition. July 1986, pp. 85–88. Subliminal messages: Subtle crime stoppers.

Chaloult, L.; Borgeat, F.; and Chabot, R. Dec. 1980. Subliminal perception. 1. Its nature and the controversy engendered. *Union Med Can,* 109 (12), 694–700.

Cheesman, J., and Merikle, P. M. Oct. 1984. Priming with and without awareness. *Perception and Psychophysics,* 36 (4), 387–95.

Chemical Engineering Progress. May 1984, pp. 44–46. Gas processing techniques: Design of gas-liquid contractors.

Chew, R. 21 Mar. 1977. Three-second spots—too slow for 1992. *Advertising Age,* 48 (12), pp. 1, 87.

Chinen, A. B.; Spielvogel, A. M.; and Farrel, D. Fall 1985. The experience of intuition. *Psychological Perspectives,* 16 (2), 186, 97.

Citrin, M. D. May 1980. The effects of subliminal oedipal stimulation on competitive performance in college males and females. *Dissertation Abstracts International,* 40 (11–B), 5399–5400.

Cooper, C., and Kline, P. Feb. 1986. An evaluation of the Defense Mechanism Test. *British Journal of Psychology,* 77 (1), 10–32.

Costello, M. Mar. 1986. The ultimate brain trip. *Omni Magazine.*

Crawford, M. A. Aug. 1985. Subliminal messaging—50s technology enjoys a rebirth. *Security Management,* 29 (8), 54–56.

Daily News Record Management. 17 Jan. 1985, pp. 2, 6. Study shows brand names still scoring.

Davis, P., and Silver, M. J. Feb. 1971. Ellipse discrimination: a psychophysical task useful for studying incidental stimulation. *Perceptual and Motor Skills,* 32 (1), 95–97.

Dean, D., and Nash, C. B. 1967. Coincident plethysmograph results under controlled conditions. *Journal of the Society of Psychical Research,* 44 (731), 1–14.

DeChenne, J. A. Oct. 1976. An experimental study to determine if a task involving psychomotor and problem solving skills can be taught subliminally. *Dissertation Abstracts International,* 37 (4–A), 1947.

Dixon, N. F. 1968. "Perception without awareness": A reply to K. M. Bainrelti-Fuchs. *Acta Psychologica* (Amsterdam, Netherlands), 28 (2), 171–80.

Dixon, N. F. 1971. *Subliminal Perception: The Nature of a Controversy.* London: McGraw-Hill.

149

Doerries, L. E., and Harcum, E. R. Aug. 1967. Long-term traces of tachistoscopic word perception. *Perceptual and Motor Skills* (U.S.) 25 (1), 25–33.

Dunham, W. R. 1984. *The Science of Vital Force.* Boston: Damrell and Upham.

Erdelyi, M. H. Nov. 1972. Role of fantasy in the Poetzl (emergency) phenomenon. *Journal of Personality and Social Psychology,* 24 (2), 186–90.

Eroelyi, M. H. 1974. A new look at the new look: Perceptual defense and vigilance. *Psychological Review,* 81, 1–25.

Faenza, V. July-Oct. 1966. Conditions of equivocity of the response in relation to the problem of "subliminal perception." *Arch Psicol Neurol Psichiatr* (Italy), 27 (4), 443–55.

Farre, M. Nov.-Dec. 1965. Degree of discernability of the stimulus and perceptive behavior. *Arch Psicol Neurol Psichiatr* (Italy), 26 (6), 566–76.

Field, G. A. 1974. The unconscious organization. *Psychoanalytic Review,* 61 (3), 333–54.

Fisher, C. 1956. Dreams, images, and perception: A study of unconscious-preconscious relationships. *Journal of the American Psychoanalytic Association,* 4–48.

Fisher, C. B.; Glenwick, D. S.; and Blumenthal, R. S. Aug. 1986. Subliminal oedipal stimuli and competitive performance: An investigation of between-groups effects and mediating subject variables. *Journal of Abnormal Psychology,* 95 (3), 292–24.

Fisher, S. Aug. 1975. State Univ. New York. Effects of messages reported to be out of awareness upon the body boundary. *Journal of Nervous and Mental Disease,* 161 (2), 90–99.

Florek, W. G. Nov. 1985. An investigation of the effects of stimulating symbiotic fantasies in primipara females. *Dissertation Abstracts International,* 46 (5–B), 1720.

Folio: The Magazine for Magazine Management, Sept. 1982, pp. 32, 34. 'Subliminal synergism'—harmonized color schemes between an ad and facing editorial copy—attacts advertisers to *New Woman* magazine.

Food Technology, Feb. 1981, p. 59. Bureau of Alcohol, Tobacco and Firearms has proposed regulations governing wine, distilled spirits, and malt beverage labeling and advertising.

Foster, R. P. Apr. 1982. The effects of subliminal tachistoscopic presentation of drive-related stimuli on the cognitive functioning of paranoid and nonparanoid schizophrenics. *Dissertation Abstracts International,* 42 (10–B), 4190–91.

Frauman, D. C.; Lynn, S. J.; Hardaway, R.; and Molteni, A. Nov. 1984. Effect of subliminal symbiotic activation on hypnotic rapport and susceptibility. *Journal of Abnormal Psychology,* 93 (4), 481–483.

Fribourg, A. Sept. 1979. The effect of fantasies of merging with a good-mother figure on schizophrenic pathology. *Dissertation Abstracts International,* 40 (3–B), 1363.

Friedman, S. 1976. Perceptual registration of the analyst outside of awareness. *Psychoanalytic Quarterly,* 45 (1), 128–30.

Frith, U. July 1972. The Georgian School of Psychology: Impressions from a visit to Tbilisi. *Bulletin of the British Psychological Society,* 25 (88), 197–201.

Froufe, T. M., and Sierra, D.B. June 1985. Perception without awareness. *Boletin de Psicologia* (Spain), 7, 7–50.

Fulford, P. F. Oct. 1980. The effect of subliminal merging stimuli on test anxiety. *Dissertation Abstracts International,* 41 (4–B), 1503.

Gade, P. A., and Gertman, David. "Listening to compressed speech: The effects of instructions, experience and preference." *U.S. Army Research Institute for the Behavioral and Social Science,* Aug. 1979, TP 369.

Ganovski, L. 1977. The role of peripheral perceptions in solving mental tasks. *Activitas Nervosa Superior,* 19 (4), 280–81.

Geisler, C. J. May 1983. A new experimental method for the study of the psychoanalytic concept of repression. *Dissertation Abstracts International,* 43 (11–B), 3757.

Giddan, N. S. Mar. 1967. Recovery through images of briefly flashed stimuli. *Journal Personal Social Psychology* (U.S.), 35 (1), 1–19.

Giovacchini, P. L. 1984. The quest for dependent autonomy. *International Forum for Psychoanalysis,* 1 (2), 153–66.

Glaser, M., and Chi, J. 5 Nov. 1984. More competition, slower growth ahead for drug chains/employee theft an epidemic'': Loss prevention chief. *Drug Topics,* 128 (21), 84–85.

Glover, E. D. Mar. 1978. The influence of subliminal perception on smoking behavior. *Dissertation Abstracts International,* 38 (9–A), 5265.

151

Golland, J. H. 1967. The effects of experimental drive arousal on response to subliminal stimulation. *Dissertation Abstracts International,* 27 (11–B), 4123.

Gordon, W. K. May 1983. Combination of cognitive group therapy and subliminal stimulation in treatment of test-anxious college males. *Dissertation Abstracts International,* 43 (11–B), 3731.

Grant, R. H. Aug. 1980. The effects of subliminally projected visual stimuli on skill development, selected attention, and participation in racquetball by college students. *Dissertation Abstracts International,* 41 (2–A), 585.

Groeger, J. A. Feb. 1986. Predominant and nonpredominant analysis: Effects of level of presentation. *British Journal of Psychology,* 77 (1), 109–16.

Guthrie, G., and Wiener, M. June 1966. Subliminal perception or perception of partial cue with pictorial stimuli. *Journal Personal Social Psychology* (U.S.), 3 (6), 619–22.

Guttman, G., and Ganglberger, J. 1967. Conditioned verbal reactions triggered by subliminal thalmic stimulation. *Zeitschrift Fur Experimentelle und Angewandte Psychologie,* 14 (3), 542–44.

Haberstroh, J. 17 Sept. 1984. Can't ignore subliminal ad changes. *Advertising Age,* 55 (61), 3, 442, 44.

Hall, E. Feb. 1986. *Psychology Today,* 20 (6), 46.

Halpern, S. 1985. *Sound Health.* San Francisco: Harper and Row.

Hayden, B., and Silverstein, R. 1983. The effects of tachistoscopic oedipal stimulation on competitive dart throwing. *Psychological Research Bulletin,* Lund Univ., 23 (1), 12.

Heilbrun, K. S. Oct. 1980. The effects of subliminally presented oedipal stimuli on competitive performance. *Dissertation Abstracts International,* 41 (4–B), 1506.

Heilbrun, K. S. Apr. 1982. Reply to Silverman. *Journal of Abnormal Psychology,* 91 (2), 134–35.

Henley, S. H., and Dixon, N. F. Nov. 1974. Laterality differences in the effect of incidental stimuli upon evoked imagery. *British Journal of Psychology,* 65 (4), 529–36.

Henley, S. H., and Dixon, N. F. June 1976. Preconscious processing in schizophrenics: An exploratory investigation. *British Journal Medical Psychology,* 49 (2), 161–6.

Henley, S. R. Mar. 1984. Unconscious perception revisited: A comment on Merikle's (1982) paper. *Bulletin of the Psychonomic Society,* 22 (2), 121–24.

Herrick, R. M. Oct. 1973. Increment thresholds for multiple identical flashes in the peripheral retina. *Journal of the Optical Society of America,* 63 (10), 1261–65.

Hines, K. S. May 1978. Subliminal psychodynamic activation of oral dependency conflicts in a group of hospitalized male alcoholics. *Dissertation Abstracts International,* 38 (11–B), 5572.

Hoban, P. July 1984. Subliminal software. *Omni,* 6 (1), 30.

Hodorowski, L. Feb. 1986. The symbiotic fantasy as a therapeutic agent: An experimental comparison of the effects of four symbiotic contexts on manifest pathology in differentiated schizophrenics. *Dissertation Abstracts International,* 46 (8–B), 2810.

Hoffman, J. S. June 1986. Review of the subliminal psychodynamic activation method. Doctor of Psychology research paper, Biola Univ.

Hovsepian, W., and Quatman, G. Feb. 1978. Effects of subliminal stimulation on masculinity-femininity ratings of a male model. *Perceptual and Motor Skills,* 46(1), 155–61.

Hull, E. I. Oct. 1976. Ego states characteristic of enhanced utilization of subliminal registrations. *Dissertation Abstracts International,* 37 (4–B), 1903–04.

Impact Newsletter, 1 Sept. 1984, pp. 8–9. News notes: The Bureau of Alcohol, Tobacco and Firearms (BATF).

Jennings, L. B., and George, S. G. Dec. 1975. Perceptual vigilance and defense revisited: Evidence against Blum's psychoanalytic theory of subliminal perception. *Perceptual and Motor Skills,* 41 (3), 723–29.

Jus, A., and Jus, K. 1967. Neurophysiologic studies of the "unconscious" (thresholds of perception and elements of the "unconscious" in the production of conditioned reflexes). *Zh Nevropatol Psikhiatr (USSR), 67 (12), 1809–15.*

Kaley, H. W. Oct. 1970. The effects of subliminal stimuli and drive on verbal responses and dreams. *Dissertation Abstracts International,* 31 (4–B), 2284.

Kaplan, M. J. May 1984. The cassette connection: 127 hours and 6 minutes to a new you. *Cosmopolitan,* 197 (4), 136.

153

Kaplan, R. B. Sept. 1976. The symbiotic fantasy as a therapeutic agent: An experimental comparison of the effects of three symbiotic elements on manifest pathology in schizophrenics. *Dissertation Abstracts International,* 37 (3–B), 1437–38.

Kato, Y. Aug. 1965. *Perspectives of New Look Psychology.* Shinrigaku Kenkyu (Japan), 36 (3), 140–54.

Kaye, M. M. Sept. 1975. The therapeutic value of three merging stimuli for male schizophrenics. *Dissertation Abstracts International,* 36 (3–B), 1438–39.

Kennedy, R. S. Apr. 1971. A comparison of performance on visual and auditory monitoring tasks. *Human Factors,* 13 (2), 93–97.

Klaine, J. July 1980. Subliminal world. *Petersen's Photographic Magazine,* 9 (8), 45.

Kleespies, P., and Wiener, M. Aug. 1972. The "orienting reflex" as an input indicator in "subliminal" perception. *Perceptual and Motor Skills,* 35 (1), 103–10.

Klein, G. S.; Spence, D. P.; Holt, R. R.; and Gourevitch, S. 1958. Cognition without awareness: Subliminal influences upon conscious thought. *Journal of Abnormal Social Psychology,* 54.

Klein, S., and Moricz, E. 1969. A study of the effect of threshold stimuli. *Magyar Pszichologiai Szemle,* 26 (2), 198–206.

Kleinbrook, W. L. Feb. 1985. Pastoral considerations regarding the use of subliminal psychodynamic activation. *Dissertation Abstracts International,* 45 (8–A), 2555.

Kolers, P. A. Sept. 1972. Subliminal stimulation in simple and complex cognitive processes. *Dissertation Abstracts International,* 33 (3–B), 1269.

Kostandov, E. A. Nov.-Dec. 1985. Current significance of the work of G.V. Gershuni on subsensory reactions. *Zh Vyssh Nerv Deiat* (USSR), 35 (6), 1014–21.

Kostandov, E. A. 1969. The effect of emotional excitation on auditory threshold and subliminal reactions. *Zh Vyssh Nerv Deiat* (USSR), 19 (3), 462–70.

Kostandov, E. A. 1973. The effect of negative emotions on perception. *Voprosy Psikhologii* (USSR), 19 (6), 60–72.

Kostandov, E. A. May-June 1968. The effect of unrecognized emotional verbal stimuli. *Zh Vyssh Nerv Deiat* (USSR), 19 (3), 371–80.

Kostandov, E. A., and D'iachkova, G. I. Mar.-Apr. 1971. Evoked potentials of the human cerebral cortex to recognized and unrecognized auditory signals. *Neirofiziologiia* (USSR), 3 (2), 115–22.

Kostandov, E. A. Mar.-Apr. 1970. Perception and subliminal reactions to unrecognized stimuli. *Zh Vyssh Nerv Deiat* (USSR), 20 (2), 441–9.

Kramer, J. Sept.-Nov. 1986. Psychic guide. In *Subliminal Persuasion, Becoming All You Can Be,* pp. 33–36.

Krass, P. Spring 1980–81. Computers that would program people. *Business and Society Review,* 37, 62–64.

Krass, P. Jan. 1981. You will read this article. *Output,* 1 (11), 36–38.

Kreitler, H., and Kreitler, S. Dec. 1974. Optimization of experimental ESP results. *Journal of Parapsychology,* 38, 383–92.

Kreitler, H., and Kreitler, S. Sept. 1973. Subliminal perception and extrasensory perception. *Journal of Parapsychology,* 37 (3), 163–88.

Krishna, S. R. Sept. 1985. A review of the PA India conference. *Journal of Parapsychology,* 49 (3), 249–55.

Lander, E. Feb. 1981. In through the out door. *Omni,* 3 (6), 44.

Lasaga, J. I., and Lasaga, A. M. Aug. 1973. Sleep learning and progressive blurring of perception during sleep. *Perceptual and Motor Skills* (U. S.), 37 (1), 51–6.

Leiter, E. Feb. 1974. A study of the effects of subliminal activation of merging fantasies in differentiated and nondifferentiated schizophrenics. *Dissertation Abstracts International,* 34 (8–B) 4022–23.

Leiter, E. 1982. The effects of subliminal activation of aggressive and merging fantasies in differentiated and nondifferentiated schizophrenics. *Psychological Research Bulletin,* Lund Univ., 22 (7), 21.

Levine, A. Feb. 1986. The great subliminal self-help hoax. *New Age Magazine.*

Levy, S. Apr. 1984. The selling of subliminal. *Popular Computing,* 8 (6), 70, 75–78.

Levenson, R. W. Mar. 1983. Personality research and psychophysiology: General considerations. *Journal of Research in Personality,* 17(1), 1–21.

Lindeman, M. L. Mar. 1985. Suggestion in education: The historical path of suggestopedia. *Journal of Evolutionary Psychology,* 6 (1–2), 107–18.

Lodl, C. M. Mar. 1981. The effects of subliminal stimuli of aggressive content upon the analytic/field-independent cognitive style. *Dissertation Abstracts International,* 41 (9–B), 3559–60.

Lomangino, L. F. 1969. Depiction of subliminally and supraliminally presented aggressive stimuli and its effects on the cognitive functioning of schizophrenics. *Dissertation Abstracts International,* 30 (4–B), 1900–01.

Lombard, J. Sept. 1979. Advertising elements: Translating theory into practice, 11 (1), 4–6.

Lorenzo, G. J. Jan.-Feb. 1985. Estimulacion subliminal y diagnostico psicopatologico. Psiquis: Revista de Psiquiatria, *Psicologia y Psicosomatica,* 6 (1), 30–40.

Lozanov, G. 1971. *Suggestology.* Sophia: Nauki i Izkustvi.

Lozanov, G. 1978. *Suggestology and Outlines of Suggestopedy.* New York: Gordon and Breach.

Magri, M. B. Aug. 1979. Effects of sexual guilt upon affective responses to subliminal sexual stimuli. *Dissertation Abstracts International,* 40 (2–B), 926.

Maloney, J. C. Jan. 1983. Some psychoanalytic aspects of coronary prone behavior. *Dissertation Abstracts International,* 43 (7–B), 346.

Marketing Communications, Nov. 1978, pp. 20–26. Games corporations play: Sponsor a sports event.

Martin, A. Dec. 1975. The effect of subliminal stimulation of symbiotic fantasies on weight loss in obese women receiving behavioral treatment. *Dissertation Abstracts International,* 36 (6–B), 30354–55.

McGinley, L. 1 Jan. 1986. Uncle Sam believes messages about mom help calm nerves. *Wall Street Journal.*

McGreen, P. J. May 1986. The effects of father absence on affective responses to subliminal symbiotic messages. *Dissertation Abstracts International,* 46 (11–B), 4021–22.

McNulty, J. A.; Deckrill, F. J.; and Levy, B. A. Mar. 1967. The subthreshold perception of stimulus-meaning. *American Journal of Psychology* (U. S.), 90 (1), 28–40.

Mendelsohn, E. M. Sept. 1981. The effects of stimulating symbiotic fantasies on manifest pathology in schizophrenics: A reverse formulation. *Journal of Nervous and Mental Disease,* 169 (9), 580–90.

Mendelsohn, E. M. June 1980. Responses of schizophrenic men to subliminal psychodynamic stimuli. *Dissertation Abstracts International,* 40 (12–B), 5820–21.

156

Merikle, P. M. Mar. 1982. Unconscious perception revisited. *Perception and Psychophysics,* 31 (3), 298–301.

Miller, W. J. 1982. Descent into Heller: Mythic imagery in *Catch-22. Journal of Mental Imagery,* 6 (2), 145–56.

Mitchell, M. S. June 1985. The effects of subliminally presented praise and reprobation stimuli on willingness to self-disclose. *Dissertation Abstracts International,* 45 (12–B), 3986.

Mofield, J. P. Mar. 1986. Response of blood pressure to relaxation and subliminal suggestion. *Dissertation Abstracts International,* 46 (9–A), 2632.

Molfese, D. Nov. 1985. When is a word a word? *Psychology Today.*

Monakhov, K. K., and Kamenskaia, V. M. 1980. Status of Neurophysiologic research in psychiatry. *Zh Nevropatol Psikhiatr,* 80 (4), 560–64.

Moore, T. E. Spring 1982. Subliminal advertising: What you see is what you get. *Journal of Marketing,* 46 (2), 38–47.

Moore, T. E. July 1985. Subliminal delusion. *Psychology Today,* 19 (2), 10.

Mopiarty, J. B. 1968. Cognitive functioning of schizophrenics as affected by aggressive stimuli subliminally and supraliminally presented. *Dissertation Abstracts International* , 29 (2–B), 775.

Morgan, P., and Morgan, D.L. 1988. *Subliminal Research: Bibliography and Review.* Center for Independent Research, Clarion Univ.

Moroney, E., and Bross, M. Feb. 1984. Effect of subliminal visual material on an auditory signal detection task. *Perceptual and Motor Skills,* 58 (1), 103–13.

Morrison, A. P. 1982. Reflections on "unconscious oneness fantasies." *International Forum for Psychoanalysis,* 1 (2), 167–80.

Morse, R. C., and Stoller, D. Sept. 1982. The hidden message that breaks habits. *Science Digest,* 90 (1), 28.

Mullins, W. W. Apr. 1978. Convexity theorem for subthreshold stimuli in linear models of visual contrast detection. *Journal of the Optical Society of America,* 68 (4), 456–59.

Muse, D. Apr. 1984. Expando-vision: User-friendly manipulations? *Microcomputing,* 8 (2), 64.

Mykel, N. B. Feb. 1977. Emergence of unreported stimuli into imagery as a function of laterality of presentation. *Dissertation Abstracts International,* 37 (8–B), 4156.

Nachmies, D. Mar. 1981. Subliminal politics. *Annals of American Academic Politics and Social Science,* 454 (2), 230.

Newsday. 8 Jan. 1987. Will moving to Seattle take Muzak out of the elevator?

Nissenfeld, S. M. Jan. 1980. The effects of four tapes of subliminal stimuli on female depressives. *Dissertation Abstracts International,* 40 (7–B), 3412–13.

Novomeysky, A. Mar. 1984. On the possible effect of an experimenter's subliminal or telepathic influence on dermo-optic sensitivity. *PSI Research,* 3 (1), 8–15.

Oberlander, R. Mar. 1979. Beauty in a hospital aids the cure. *Hospitals,* 53 (6), 89–92.

Olson, M. C. Mar. 1975. Subliminal messages in advertising. Paper presented at the Annual Meeting of the Conference on English Education (13th, Colorado Springs, Colo., Mar. 20–22, 1975).

Ostrander, S., and Schroeder, L. 1980. *Superlearning.* New York: Delta.

Ostrander, S., and Schroeder, L. 1985. *Subliminal Report.* New York: Superlearning.

Output. Jan. 1981, pp. 36–38. Experiments in subliminal communication continue.

Packard, V. Feb. 1981. The new (and still hidden) persuaders. *Reader's Digest,* 118 (4), 120.

Packer, S. B. July 1984. The effect of subliminally stimulating fantasies aimed at gratifying symbiotic and sanctioning aggressive strivings on assertiveness difficulties in women. *Dissertation Abstracts International,* 459 (1–B), 361.

Palmatier, J. R. Jan. 1981. The effects of subliminal stimulation of symbiotic fantasies on the behavior therapy treatment of smoking. *Dissertation Abstracts International,* 41 (7–B), 2774–75.

Paper, Film and Foil Converter. Oct. 1985, pp. 100–104. Spaghetti and tomato sauces—why not aseptics?

Parker, K. A. June 1978. The effects of subliminal merging stimuli on the academic performance of college students. *Dissertation Abstracts International,* 38 (12–B), 6168.

Philpott, A., and Wilding, J. Nov. 1979. Semantic interference from subliminal stimuli in a dichoptic viewing situation. *British Journal of Psychology,* 70 (4), 559–63.

Powell, R. C. Apr. 1979. The "subliminal" versus the "subconscious" in the American acceptance of psychoanalysis, 1906–1910. *Journal History Behavioral Science,* 15 (2), 155–65.

Public Relations Journal. Sept. 1984, pp. 18–20. Pacific Bell's Low-Key Approach to Olympic Sponsorship.

Pushkash, M. June 1981. Effect of the content of visual presented subliminal stimulation on semantic and figural learning task performance. *Dissertation Abstracts International,* 41 (12–A), 5036.

Rees, W. J. Nov. 1971. On the terms "subliminal perception" and "subception." *British Journal of Psychology,* 62 (4), 501–4.

Richardson, M. V. Dec. 1981. The effects of subliminal implantation in written material on the decision-making process. *Dissertation Abstracts International,* 42 (6–A), 2592.

Robertson, S. R. May 1983. The effect of subliminal merging stimuli on field dependence. *Dissertation Abstracts International,* 43 (11–B), 3741.

Rohrer, D. M. Mar. 1977. A rationality standard for the first amendment. Paper presented at the Annual Meeting of the Eastern Communication Association (New York City, 24–26 Mar. 1977).

Roll, W. G., and de A. Montagno, E. July 1985. System theory, neurophysiology and psi. International Conference on Parapsychology: Eastern and Western perspectives (1985, Waltair, India). *Journal of Indian Psychology,* 4 (2), 43–84.

Romberg, L. 1975. *Workings of Your Mind.* Burlington, Ontario: Audio Cybernetics.

Roney-Dougal, S. July-Aug. 1981. The interface between psi and subliminal perception. *Parapsychology Review,* 12 (4), 12–18.

Rose, C. 1985. *Accelerated Learning.* Great Britain.

Ross, D. L. Dec. 1978. The effects of subliminal oedipal stimulation on competitive performance in college men. *Dissertation Abstracts International,* 39 (6–B), 3005.

Roufs, J. A., and Pellegrino Van Stuyvenberg, J. A. 1976. Gain curve of the eye to subliminal sinusoidal modulation. *IPO Annual Progress Report,* 11, 56–63.

Ruzumna, J. S. 1969. The effect of cognitive control on responsiveness to subliminal stimulation in social situations. *Dissertation Abstracts International,* 30 (1–B), 373–74.

Saegert, J. Feb. 1979. Another look at subliminal perception. *Journal of Advertising Research,* 19 (1), 55–57.

Sandler, C. 19 Feb. 1985. Mind altering software: Do you want to trance? *PC,* 4 (1), 42.

Schmeidler, G. 1986. Subliminal perception and ESP: Order in diversity? *The Journal of the American Society of Psychical Research,* 80 (3).

Schwartz, M., and Rem, M. A. July 1975. Does the averaged evoked response encode subliminal perception? *Psychophysiology,* 12 (4), 390–94.

Shah, P. M. Oct. 1981. The time course of temporal summation at various background luminances. *Dissertation Abstracts International,* 42 (4–B), 1660.

Shapiro, T. 1978. On the verification of psychoanalytic concepts by extraclinical techniques. *International Journal Psychoanalytic Psychotherapy,* 7, 586–601.

Shevrin, H.; Smith, W. H.; Fitzler, D. E. Mar. 1971. Average evoked response and verbal correlates of unconscious mental processes. *Psychophysiology,* 8 (2), 149–62.

Shevrin, H. 1973. Brain wave correlates of subliminal stimulation, unconscious attention, primary- and secondary-process thinking, and repressiveness. *Psychological Issues,* 8 (2), Mono. 30) 56–87.

Shevrin, H. July 1975. Does the average evoked response encode subliminal perception? Yes. A reply to Schwartz and Rem. *Psychology* 12 (4), 395–98.

Shevrin, H., and Dickman, S. May 1980. The psychological unconscious: A necessary assumption for all psychological theory? *American Psychologist,* 35 (5), 421–34.

Shevrin, H. May 1976. Rapaport's contribution to research: A look to the future. *Bulletin of the Menninger Clinic,* 40 (3), 211–28.

Shevrin, H.; Voth, H.; and Gardner, R. W. Nov. 1971. Research perspectives on treatment and diagnosis. *Bulletin of the Menninger Clinic,* 35 (6), 461–78.

Shield, P. H.; Harrow, M.; and Tucker, G. 1974. Investigation of factors related to stimulus overinclusion. *Psychiatric Quarterly* (U. S.), 48 (1), 109–16.

Shirley, L., M.D. 1987. Unpublished article. Subliminal communication discovery and development.

Silverman, L. H.; Levinson, P.; Mendelsohn, E.; Ungaro, R.; and Bronstein, A. A. Dec. 1975. A clinical application of subliminal psychodynamic activation. On the stimulation of symbiotic fantasies as an adjunct in the treatment of hospitalized schizophrenics. *Journal of Nervous and Mental Disease,* 161 (6), 379, 92.

Silverman, L. H. Nov. 1985. Comments on three recent subliminal psychodynamic activation investigations (letter). *Journal of Abnormal Psychology,* 94 (4), 640–48.

Silverman, L. H. 1980. A comprehensive report of studies using the subliminal psychodynamic activation method. *Psychological Research Bulletin,* Lund Univ., 20 (3), 22.

Silverman, L. H. 1972. Drive stimulation and psychopathology: On the conditions under which drive-related external events evoke pathological reactions. *Psychoanalysis and Contemporary Science,* 1, 306–26.

Silverman, L. H.; Spiro, R. H.; Weisbert, J. S.; and Candell, P. 1969. The effects of aggressive activation and the need to merge on pathological thinking in schizophrenia. *Journal of Nervous and Mental Disease,* 148 (1), 39–51.

Silverman, L. H., and Silverman, S. E. Feb. 1967. The effects of subliminally presented drive stimuli on the cognitive functioning of schizophrenics. *Journal of Projective Techniques Personal Assessment* (U. S.), 31 (1), 78–85.

Silverman, L. H.; Martin, A.; Ungaro, R.; and Mendelsohn, E. June 1978. Effect of subliminal stimulation of symbiotic fantasies on behavior modification treatment of obesity. *Journal of Consulting Clinical Psychology,* 46 (3), 432–41.

Silverman, L. H., and Shiro, R. H. Jan. 1963. The effects of subliminal, supraliminal and vocalized aggression on the ego functioning of schizophrenics. *Journal of Nervous and Mental Disease* (U. S.), 146 (1), 50–61.

Silverman, L. H. 1978. Further comments on matters relevant to investigations of subliminal phenomena: A reply. *Perceptual and Motor Skills,* 27 (3), 1343–50.

Silverman, L. H., and Spiro, R. H. June 1967. Further investigation of the effects of subliminal aggressive stimulation on the ego functioning of schizophrenics. *Journal of Projective Techniques Personal Assessment* (U. S.), 31 (3), 225–33.

Silverman, L. H., and Goldweber, A. M. 1966. A further study of the effects of subliminal aggressive stimulation on thinking. *Journal of Nervous and Mental Disease,* 143 (6), 463–72.

Silverman, L. H.; Lachmann, F. M.; and Milich, R. H. 1984. In response. *International Forum for Psychoanalysis,* 1 (2), 205–217.

Silverman, L. H., and Weinberger, J. Dec. 1985. Mommy and I are one. Implications for psychotherapy. *American Psychology,* 40 (12), 1296–308.

Silverman, L. H., and Candell, P. May 1970. On the relationship between aggressive activation, symbiotic merging, intactness of body boundaries, and manifest pathology in schizophrenics. *Journal Nervous and Mental Disorders,* 150 (5), 387–99.

Silverman, L. H. 1985. Research on psychoanalytic psychodynamic propositions. Special Issue: Current thinking in psychoanalysis. *Clinical Psychology Review,* 5 (3), 247–57.

Silverman, L. H., and Spiro, R. H. 1967. Some comments and data on the partial cue controversy and other matters relevant to investigations of subliminal phenomena. *Perceptual and Motor Skills,* 25 (1), 325–338.

Silverman, L. H. Apr. 1966. A technique for the study of psychodynamic relationships: the effects of subliminally presented aggressive stimuli on the production of pathological thinking in a schizophrenic population. *Journal of Consulting Psychology* (U. S.), 30 (2), 103–1.

Silverman, L. H., and Lachmann, F. M. Jan. 1985. The therapeutic properties of unconscious oneness fantasies: Evidence and treatment implications. *Contemporary Psychoanalysis,* 21 (1), 91–115.

Silverman, L. H. 1979. Two unconscious fantasies as mediators of successful psychotherapy. *Psychotherapy: Theory and Practice,* 16, 215–230.

Silverman, L. H. 1980a. Is subliminal psychodynamic activation in trouble? *Journal of Abnormal Psychology.*

Silverman, L. H. 1980b. A comprehensive report of studies using the subliminal psychodynamic activation method. *Psychological Research Bulletin,* 2 (3).

Silverman, L. H., and Candell, P. 1970. On the relationship between aggressive activation, symbiotic merging on ego functioning of schizophrenics. *Perceptual and Motor Skills,* 32, 93–94.

Silverman, L. H.; Candell, P.; Pettit, T. F.; and Blum, F. A. 1971. Further data on effects of aggressive activation and symbiotic merging on ego functioning of schizophrenics. *Perceptual and Motor Skills,* 32, 93–94.

Silverman, L. H.; Lachmann, F. M.; and Milich, R. H. 1984. Unconscious oneness fantasies: Experimental findings and implications for treatment. *International Forum for Psychoanalysis,* 1 (2).

Silverman, L. H.; Levinson, P.; Mendelsohn, E.; Ungaro, R.; and Bronstein, A. 1975. A clinical application of subliminal psychodynamic activation: On the stimulation of symbiotic fantasies as an adjunct in the treatment of hospitalized schizophrenics. *Journal of Nervous and Mental Disease,* 161, 379–392.

Silverman, L. H. Apr. 1979. The unconscious fantasy as therapeutic agent in psychoanalytic treatment. *Journal of American Academic Psychoanalysis,* 7 (2), 189–218.

Silverman, L. H.; Lachmann, F. M.; and Milich, R. H. 1984. Unconscious oneness fantasies: Experimental findings and implications for treatment. *International Forum for Psychoanalysis,* 1 (2), 107–52.

Skean, S. R. May 1978. Videotape presentation of subliminal stimulation based on galvanic skin response monitoring: An investigation in counselor education. *Dissertation Abstracts International,* 38 (11–A), 6547.

Smith, C. D. Dec. 1982. Effects of subliminal stimulation on creative thinking. *Dissertation Abstracts International,* 43 (6–B), 2004.

Smith, R. B. Apr. 1979. The effects of the incidental perception of rhythm on task performance and mood. *Dissertation Abstracts International,* 39 (10–B), 5049–50.

Soap/Cosmetics/Chemical Specialties. Aug. 1984, pp. 34–36. The growing importance of fragrance in functional products.

Sokolov, A. N. 1968. *Internal speech and thinking.* Moscow, USSR: Prosveshchenie.

Spence, D. P., and Gordon, C. M. 1973. Activation and assessment of an early oral fantasy: An exploratory study.

Spence, D. P., and Gordon, C. M. 1967. Activation and measurement of an early oral fantasy: An exploratory study. *Journal of the American Psychoanalytic Association,* 15 (1), 99–129.

163

Spence, D. P. and Smith, G. J. Aug. 1977. Experimenter bias against subliminal perception? Comments on a replication. *British Journal of Psychology,* 68 (3), 279–80.

Spiro, R. H., and Silverman, L. H. 1969. Effects of body awareness and aggressive activation on ego functioning of schizophrenics. *Perceptual and Motor Skills,* 28 (2), 575–85.

Spiro, T. W. May 1976. The effects of subliminal symbiotic stimulation and strengthening self boundaries of schizophrenic pathology. *Dissertation Abstracts International,* 36 (11–B), 5818–19.

Stambrook, M., and Martin, D. G. 1983. Brain laterality and the subliminal perception of facial expression. *International Journal Neuroscience,* 18 (1–2), 45–58.

Steele, E. H. Oct. 1969. The impact of psychoanalytic theory on the freedom of speech. *Psychoanalyst Quarterly* (U. S.), 38 (4), 583–615.

Stoller, R. J. Aug. 1976. Sexual excitement. *Archives of General Psychiatry,* 33 (8), 899–909.

Strauss, H. 1968. A phenomenological approach to the subconscious. *Nordisk Psykologi,* 20 (4), 203–6.

Strickland, R. G. Oct. 1976. Microgenesis of subjective meaning in visual perception. *Dissertation Abstracts International,* 37 (4–B), 1931.

Stross, L., and Shevrin, H. Jan. 1969. Hypnosis as a method for investigating unconscious thought processes. A review of research. *Journal of American Psychoanalytic Assoc* (U.S.), 17 (1), 100–135.

Stross, L., and Shervin, H. 1968. Thought organization in hypnosis and the waking state. *Journal of Nervous and Mental Disease,* 147 (3), 272–88.

Sutphen, D. 1982. Battle for Your Mind (Transcript from speech delivered to World Congress of Hypnotists). Malibu, Calif.: Valley of the Sun Publishing.

Swanson, R. J. May 1981. The effects of oedipally related stimuli in the subliminal psychodynamic activation paradigm: A replication and an extension. *Dissertation Abstracts International,* 41 (11–B), 4279.

Taris, L. J. Nov. 1970. Subliminal perception: An experimental study to determine whether a science concept can be taught subliminally to fourth grade pupils. *Dissertation Abstracts International,* 31 (5–A), 2199.

164

Taylor, E. Sept. 1985. Brain Washing. Radio broadcast transcript. (Transcript available: JAR Publishing.)

Taylor, E. Nov. 1987. Cancer remission. Mind Mint Memo. Salt Lake City, JAR, Inc.

Taylor, E. Nov. 1987. Miss Utah utilizes subliminal training. Mind Mint Memo, JAR, Inc., Salt Lake City.

Taylor, E. Oct. 1987. Cats obeying win suggestion. *Deseret News* article. Author: L. Benson.

Taylor, E. 14 Sept. 1987. Inaudible messages making a noise. Comments in *Insight Magazine.* Author: S. Dillingham.

Taylor, E. 29 Jan. 1987. "Silent" voices: Can subliminal tapes change your life? *Deseret News.* Author: E. Jarvik.

Taylor, E. July 1986. Holistic approach to hypnosis. *Attain.* Springfield, Louisiana.

Thompson, A. H.; Dewar, R. E.; and Franken, R. E. June 1971. A test of the set disruption interpretation of perceptual defense. *Canadian Journal of Psychology* (Canada), 25 (3), 222–27.

Thompson, M. D. Sept. 1980. Technology as a craft of deceit. *USA Today,* 109 (4), 16.

Thuerer, J. R. Apr. 1985 Computer-assisted spelling: A subliminal methodology to increase cognitive performance and academic self-concept. *Dissertation Abstract International,* 45 (10–A), 3074.

Tomlinson, K. Jan. 1983. Just snore that weight off. Los Angeles, 28 (2), 206.

Trank, D. M. 1976. Subliminal Stimulation: Hoax or Reality? Study prepared at Univ. of Iowa.

Trewin, I. Jan. 6, 1984. Auberon Waugh: Subliminal plagiarism for *Lord of the Flies? Publishers Weekly,* 225 (1), 22.

Trieber, E. J. Aug. 1984. The effects of supraliminal stimulation combined with subliminal symbiotic stimuli on academic performance. *Dissertation Abstracts International,* 45 (2–B), 688–89.

Trimble, R., and Eriksen, C. W. 1966. "Subliminal cues" and the Muller-type illusion. *Perception and Psychophysics,* 1 (11), 401–4.

The Truth about Subliminals. 1985. St. Paul, Minn.: Llewellyn Publications

Udolf, R. 1981. *Handbook of Hypnosis for Professionals.*

165

Ungaro, R. Apr. 1982. The role of ego strength and alternative subliminal messages in behavioral treatment of obesity. *Dissertation Abstracts International,* 42 (10–B), 4215–16.

Unknown, Feb. 28, 1985. Ads against wall in video background. *Advertising Age,* p. 6.

Unknown, 1985. Can you sell subliminal messages to consumers? *Journal of Advertising,* 14 (3), 59–60.

Unknown, Dec. 9, 1985. Dristan ads are blatantly subliminal. *Marketing,* 90 (49), 2.

Unknown, June 5, 1985. If this fails, try smashing the bug with the flat end of the radio. *Wall Street Journal,* 3 Star, Eastern (Princeton, N.J.) Edition, 205 (109), 33.

Unknown, Jan. 7, 1985. Sidelights: Subliminal/videos. *Television/Radio Age,* 32 (13), 96.

Unknown, Oct. 1985. Subliminal advertising: Do messages lurk in the shadows? *Food and Beverage Marketing,* 4 (10), 42.

Unknown, Nov. 18, 1985. Subliminal advertising: Fact or fantasy. *Advertising Compliance Service,* 5 (22), 4–7.

Unknown, Dec. 2, 1985. Subliminal advertising: Fact or fantasy. *Advertising Compliance Service,* 5 (23), 8–12.

Unknown, Apr. 1985. Subliminal messages come out of the closet. *Progressive Grocer,* 64 (4), 6,10.

Unknown, Apr. 1985. Subliminal testing: 25 years later. *Marketing Communications,* p. 8.

Vilenskaya, L. June 1985. Firewalking and beyond. *PSI Research,* 4 (2), 89–109.

Vilenskaya, L. 1984. My view of psi in criminology: Interview with Ron Nolan. *PSI Research,* 3 (3–4), 118–30.

Vroon, P. A. 1985. From radio metaphor to computer metaphor: Publication trends in psychology. Gedrag: *Tijdschrift voor Psychologie,* 13 (6), 1–9.

Walker, A. Dec. 1979. Music and the unconscious. *British Medical Journal,* 2 (6205), 1641–43.

Walker, P., and Meyer, R. R. May 1978. The subliminal perception of movement and the course of autokinesis. *British Journal of Psychology,* 69 (2), 225–31.

Wall Street Journal. 3 Star, Eastern (Princeton, N.J.) Edition, Aug. 16, 1984, p. 27. Company-built retreats reflect firms' cultures and personalities.

Wall Street Journal. 3 Star, Eastern SP Edition, Apr. 17, 1979, pp. 1, 35. Retailers increasingly use sensual impressions to build sales.

Wall Street Journal. 3 Star, Eastern (Princeton, N.J.) Edition, Sept. 30, 1983, p. 33. Simutech has introduced a device to change behavior by subliminal suggestion.

West, G. N. July 1985. The effects of auditory subliminal psychodynamic activation on state anxiety. *Dissertation Abstracts International,* 46 (1–B), 319.

Westerlundh, B. 1985. Subliminal influence on imagery: Two exploratory experiments. *Psychological Research Bulletin,* Lund Univ., 24 (6–7), 31.

Whalen, B. Mar. 1985. 'Threshold messaging' touted as antitheft measure. *Marketing News,* 19 (6), 5–6.

Whittaker, R. 1975. Subliminal perception: Myth or magic? *Educational Broadcasting,* 8 (6), 17–22.

Wiener, M., and Kleespies, P. Dec. 1968. Some comments and data on partial cue controversy and other matters relevant to investigations of subliminal phenomena: A rejoinder. *Perceptual and Motor Skills* (U. S.), 27 (3), 847–56.

Wilson, G. T. Oct. 1973. Effects of false feedback on avoidance behavior: "Cognitive" desensitization revisited. *Journal of Personality and Social Psychology,* 28 (1), 115–22.

Winnett, R. L. Dec. 1981. The comparative effects of literal metaphorical subliminal stimulation on the activation of oedipal fantasies in dart-throwing performance and word recall tasks. *Dissertation Abstracts International,* 42 (6–B), 2557.

Worchel, S., and Yohai, S. M. Jan. 1979. The role of attribution in the experience of crowding. *Journal of Experimental Social Psychology,* 15 (1), 91–104.

Worthington, A. G. June 1966. Generalization phenomena associated with previous pairings of UCS (shock) and subliminal visual stimuli. *Journal of Personal Social Psychology* (U.S.), 3 (6), 634–4.

Worthington, A. G., and Dixon, N. F. 1968. Subthreshold perception of stimulus meaning. *American Journal of Psychology,* 81 (3), 453–56.

Zingirian, M.; Molfino, A.; Levialdi, S.; and Trillo, M. 1971. Monocular and binocular responses to liminal and subliminal stimuli. *Ophthalmologica* (Switzerland), 162 (1), 41–50.

167

BIBLIOGRAPHY

Advertising Age. 28 Feb. 1985, p. 6. Ads against wall in video background.

Advertising Age. 14 June 1982, p. 63. *New Woman* magazine has developed what it calls 'subliminal synergism,' a technique whereby the dominant color or colors of a four-color ad page are picked up on the page opposite as a color-coded tint block behind a headline.

Andersson, A.L.; Fries, I.; and Smith, G.J. 1970. Change in after-image and spiral aftereffect serials due to anxiety caused by subliminal threat. *Scandinavian Journal of Psychology,* 11 (1), 7–17.

Antell, J.J., and Goldberger, L. 1978. The effects of subliminally presented sexual and aggressive stimuli on literary creativity. *Psychological Research Bulletin,* Lund Univ., 19 (7), 20.

Ariam, S., and Siller, J. Oct. 1982. Effects of subliminal oneness stimuli in Hebrew on academic performance of Israeli high school students: further evidence on the adaptation-enhancing effects of symbiotic fantasies in another culture using another language. *Journal of Abnormal Psychology,* 91 (5), 343–49.

Aurell, C. G. Oct. 1979. Perception: A model comprising two modes of consciousness. *Perceptual and Motor Skills,* 49 (2), 431–44.

Bach, R. 1973. *Jonathan Livingston Seagull.* New York: Avon Books.

Barchas, P. R., and Perlaki, K. M. June 1986. Processing of pre-consciously acquired information measured by hemispheric asymmetry and selection accuracy. *Behav Neurosci,* 100 (3), 343–49.

Barenklau, K. E. Dec. 1981. Using subliminals in technical training. *Training,* 18 (1), 50–51.

169

Barkoczi, I.; Sera, L.; and Komlosi, A. Mar. 1983. Relationships between functional asymmetry of the hemispheres, subliminal perception, and some defense mechanisms in various experimental settings. *Psychologia: An International Journal of Psychology in the Orient,* 26 (1), 1–20.

Bartoo, P. 1988. Transformations: The Healing Arts in Santa Fe. Special Supplement to the *Santa Fe Reporter.*

Bauer, W. Feb. 1986. The effects of conditional and unconditional subliminal symbiotic stimuli on intrinsic motivation. *Dissertation Abstracts International,* 46 (8–B), 2794–95.

Beisgen, R. T., Jr.; and Gibby, R. G., Jr. 1969. Virginia Commonwealth Univ. Autonomic and verbal discrimination of a subliminally learned task. *Perceptual and Motor Skills,* 29 (2), 503–7.

Beloff, J. May 1973. The subliminal and the extrasensory. *Parapsychology Review,* 4 (3), 23–27.

Block, M. P., and Vanden Bergh, B. G. 1985. Michigan State Univ. Can you sell subliminal messages to consumers? *Journal of Advertising,* 14 (3), 59–62.

Bohm, D., and Peat, D. 1987. *Science, Order and Creativity.* New York: Bantam.

Borgeat, F., and Chaloult, L. Mar. 1985. A relaxation experiment using radio broadcasts. *Canada's Mental Health,* 33 (1), 11–13.

Borgeat, F., and Goulet, J. June 1983. Psychophysiological changes following auditory subliminal suggestions for activation and deactivation. *Perceptual and Motor Skills,* 56 (3), 759–66.

Borgeat, F. Dec. 1983. Psychophysiological effects of two different relaxation procedures: Progressive relaxation and subliminal relaxation. *Psychiatric Journal of the University of Ottawa,* 8 (4), 181–85.

Borgeat, F.; Elie, R.; Chaloult, L.; and Chabot, R. Feb. 1985. Psychophysiological responses to masked auditory stimuli. *Canadian Journal of Psychiatry,* 30 (1), 22–27.

Borgeat, F.; Chabot, R.; and Chaloult, L. June 1981. Subliminal perception and level of activation. *Canadian Journal of Psychiatry,* 26 (4), 255–59.

Borgeat, F., and Pannetier, M. F. 1982. Value of cumulative electrodermal responses in subliminal auditory perception: A preliminary study. *Encephale,* 8 (4), 487–99.

Bower, B. Fall 1986. Newsletter article, Is it all in the mind? Institute of Noetic Sciences.

170

Broadcasting. 3 Oct. 1977, pp. 31, 32. Florida trial of 'TV addict' goes on the air: A fifteen-year-old boy, R. Zamora, is being tried for first-degree murder, and his attorney, E. Rubin, is pleading that the boy is insane due to 'involuntary,' subliminal TV intoxication. Noncommercial WPBT (TV), Miami, working under the rules of a recent Florida Supreme Court opinion that TV cameras should be allowed in courtrooms as part of a year-long experiment, is broadcasting excerpts of the trial beginning at 10 each night.

Bronstein, A. A. Mar. 1983. An experimental study of internalization fantasies in schizophrenic men. *Psychotherapy: Theory, Research and Practice,* 20 (4), 408–16.

Brosgole, L., and Contino, A. F. June 1973. Intrusion of subthreshold learning upon later performance. *Psychological Reports,* 32 (3), 795–99.

Brush, J. Oct. 1982. Subliminal stimulation in asthma: Imaginal, associative, and physiological effects. *Dissertation Abstracts International,* 43 (4–B), 1294–95.

Bryant-Tuckett, R., and Silverman, L.H. July 1984. Effects of the subliminal stimulation of symbiotic fantasies on the academic performance of emotionally handicapped students. *Journal of Counseling Psychology,* 31 (3), 295–305.

Building Supply and Home Centers (formerly *Building Supply News*). Apr. 1987, pp. 88–94. Crooked employees.

Burkham, P. Apr. 1982. The effect of subliminal presentation of two gratifying fantasies on female depressives. *Dissertation Abstracts International,* 42 (10–B), 4183.

Business Week Industrial Edition. 19 May 1986, pp. 126–28. Reeling and dealing: Video meet Wall Street.

Carroll, R. T. July 1980. Neurophysiological and psychological mediators of response to subliminal perception: The influence of hemisphericity and defensive style on susceptibility to subliminally presented conflict-laden stimuli. *Dissertation Abstracts International,* 41 (1–B), 342–43.

Charman, D. K. 1979. An examination of relationship between subliminal perception, visual information processing, levels of processing, and hemispheric asymmetries. *Perceptual and Motor Skills,* 49 (2), 451–55.

Claire, J. B. 1981. A holographic model of a psychosomatic pattern: Freud's specimen dream reinterpreted. *Psychotherapy and Psychosomatics,* 36 (2), 132–42.

Cohen, R. O. Nov. 1977. The effects of four subliminally introduced merging stimuli on the psychopathology of schizophrenic women. *Dissertation Abstracts International,* 38 (5–B), 2356–57.

Computer Decisions. 29 Jan. 1985, p. 26. Suggestive software.

Cook, H. Fall 1985. Effects of subliminal symbiotic gratification and the magic of believing on achievement. *Psychoanalytic Psychology,* 2 (4), 365–71.

Cuperfain, R., and Clarke, T. K. 1985. A new perspective of subliminal perception. *Journal of Advertising,* 14 (1), 36–41.

Czyzewksa-Pacewicz, M. 1984. The priming phenomenon in semantic memory evoked by subthreshold stimuli. *Przeglad Psychologiczny,* 27 (3), 617–29.

Dauber, R. B. Feb. 1984. Subliminal psychodynamic activation in depression: On the role of autonomy issues in depressed college women. *Journal of Abnormal Psychology,* 93 (1), 9–18.

DeHaan, H. J. A speech-rate intelligibility/comprehensibility threshold for speeded and time-compressed connected speech. U.S. Army Research Institute for the Behavioral and Social Sciences, 1978 (June) TB 297.

de Martino, C. R. 1969. The effects of subliminal stimulation as a function of stimulus content, drive arcusal and priming, and defense against drive. *Dissertation Abstracts International,* 29 (12–B), 4843.

Dixon, N. F. 1981. The conscious/unconscious interface: Contributions to an understanding. *Psychological Research Bulletin,* Lund Univ., 21 (5), 15.

Dixon, N. F. 1983. Data from different areas of research are reviewed to develop a flow model to explain how physiological events in the brain give rise to representations in the mind. *Archiv fur Psychologie,* 135 (1), 55–66.

Dixon, N. F.; Henley, S. H.; and Weir, C. G. Spring 1984. Extraction of information from continuously masked successive stimuli: An exploratory study. *Current Psychological Research and Reviews,* 3 (1), 38–44.

Dixon, N. 1981. *Preconscious Processing.* New York: Wiley.

Dixon, N. F. May-June 1979. Subliminal perception and parapsychology: Points of contact. *Parapsychology Review,* 10 (3), 1–6.

Efran, J. S., and Marcia, J. E. 1967. Treatment of fears by expectancy manipulation: An exploratory investigation. *Proceedings of the 75th annual convention of the American Psychological Association,* 2, 239–40.

Ehrenwald, J. Dec. 1975. Cerebral localization and the psi syndrome. *Journal of Nervous and Mental Disease,* 161 (6), 3393–98.

Einstein, A. 1964. *Ideas and Opinions.* New York: Bonanza Books.

Emrich, H., and Heinemann, L. G. 1966. EEG with subliminal perception of emotionally significant words. *Psychologische Forschung,* 29 (4), 285–96.

Emmelkamp, P. M., and Straatman, H. 1976. A psychoanalytic reinterpretation of the effectiveness of systematic desensitization: Fact or fiction? *Behaviour Research and Therapy,* 14 (3), 245–49.

Feldman, J. B. May 1979. The utilization of the subliminal psychodynamic activation method in the further examination of conscious and unconscious measures of death anxiety. *Dissertation Abstracts International,* 39 (11–B), 5547–48.

Ferguson, M. 1985. *Brain/Mind Bulletin.* Perspective, 7 (4).

Ferguson, M. 1986. *Brain/Mind Bulletin.* Perspective, 11 (9).

Ferguson, M. Nov. 1987. Mind-body researchers meet at Big Sur 'Summit.' *Brain/Mind Bulletin.*

Fisher, S. May 1976. Conditions affecting boundary response to messages out of awareness. *Journal of Nervous and Mental Disease,* 162 (5), 313–22.

Fiss, H. Dec. 1966. The effects of experimentally induced changes in alertness on response to subliminal stimulation. *Journal of Personality and Social Psychology* (U. S.), 34 (4), 577–95.

Foodman, A. 1976. Hemispheric asymmetrical brain wave indicators of unconscious mental processes. *Journal of Operational Psychiatry,* 7 (1), 3–15.

Fox, Muriel 1966. Differential effects of subliminal and supraliminal stimulation. *Dissertation Abstracts International,* 27 (4B), 1289–90.

Freud, S. 1961. *The Future of an Illusion.* Garden City, N.Y.: Doubleday and Co.

173

Fribourg, A. June 1981. The effect of fantasies of merging with a good-mother figure on schizophrenic pathology. *Journal of Nervous and Mental Disease,* 169 (6), 337–47.

Gadlin, W., and Fiss, H. 1967. Odor as a facilitator of the effects of subliminal stimulation. *Journal of Personality and Social Psychology,* 7 (1, Pt. 1), 95–100.

Geisler, C. J. Oct. 1986. The use of subliminal psychodynamic activation in the study of repression. *Journal of Personality and Social Psychology* (U. S.), 51 (4), 844–45.

Genkina, O. A., and Shostakovich, G. S. Nov.-Dec. 1983. Elaboration of a conditioned reflex in chronic alcoholics using an unrecognizable motivationally significant word. *Zh Vyssh Nerv Deiat,* 33 (6), 1010–18.

Glennon, S. June 1984. The effects of functional brain asymmetry and hemisphericity on the subliminal activation of residual oedipal conflicts. *Dissertation Abstracts International,* 44 (12–B), 3931–32.

Gordon, C. M., and Spence, D. D. 1966. The facilitating effects of food set and food deprivation on responses to a subliminal food stimulus. *Journal of Personality,* 34Z (3), 406–15.

Greenberg, R. P., and Fisher, S. Dec. 1980. Freud's penis–baby equation: Exploratory tests of a controversial theory. *British Journal of Medical Psychology* , 53 (4), 33–42.

Groeger, J. A. Aug. 1984. Evidence of unconscious semantic processing from a forced-error situation. *British Journal of Psychology,* 75 (3), 305–14.

Guillory, W. 1988. Unpublished. Innovations Consulting, Salt Lake City, Utah.

Hardy, G. R., and Legge, D. 1968. Cross-model induction of changes in sensory thresholds. *Quarterly Journal of Experimental Psychology,* 20 (1), 20–29.

Harrison, R. H. 1970. Effect of subliminal shock conditioning on recall. *Journal of Abnormal Psychology,* 75 (1), 19–29.

Hart, L. June 1973. The effect of noxious subliminal stimuli on the modification of attitudes toward alcoholism: A pilot study. *British Journal of Addiction,* 68 (2), 87–90.

Hebb, D. O. 1955. Drives and the C.N.S. *Psychological Review,* 62, 243–254.

Henley, S. H. 1976. Responses to homophones as a function of cue words on the unattended channel. *British Journal of Psychology,* 67 (4), 559–67.

Henley, S. 1975. Cross-model effects of subliminal verbal stimuli. *Scandinavian Journal of Psychology,* 16 (1), 30–36.

Henley, S. H. Nov. 1976. Responses to homophones as a function of cue words on the unattended channel. *British Journal of Psychology,* 67 (4), 559–67.

Hines, J. Feb. 1988. Logan, Utah, *Herald Journal* article.

Hobbs, S. Sept. 1984. The effects of subliminal oedipal and symbiotic gratification fantasies on racial attitudes. *Dissertation Abstracts International,* 45 (3–B), 1018.

Holtzman, D. Nov. 1975. Recall and importations on a word test primed by a subliminal stimulus. *Dissertation Abstracts International,* 36 (5–B), 2473.

Hylton, R. L. Sept. 1979. A comparison of the effects of aural arousal on the verbal learning of normal and learning disabled elementary school pupils. *Dissertation Abstracts International,* 40 (3–B), 1393.

Jackson, J. M. Nov. 1983. A comparison of the effects of subliminally presented fantasies of merger with each parent on the pathology of male and female schizophrenics. *Dissertation Abstracts International,* 43 (5–B), 1616–17.

Jaynes, J. 1976. *The Origin of Consciousness and the Breakdown of the Bicameral Mind.* Boston: Houghton Mifflin Co.

Jeffmar, M. 1976. Ways of cognitive action: A study of syncretism, flexibility and exactness. *Psychological Research Bulletin,* Lund Univ., no. 1 (Mono Series) 47.

Journal of Advertising Research. Feb. 1979, pp. 55–57. Whether subliminal perception influences behavior is examined by J. Saegert of Univ. of Texas at San Antonio.

Kaplan, R.; Thornton, P.; and Silverman, L. Nov. 1985. Further data on the effects of subliminal symbiotic stimulation on schizophrenics. *Journal of Nervous and Mental Disease,* 173 (11), 658–66.

Kappas, J. G. 1978. *Professional Hypnotism Manual: Introducing Physical and Emotional Suggestibility and Sexuality.* Van Nuys, Calif.: Panorama Publishing Co.

Kaser, V.A. July 1986. The effects of an auditory subliminal message upon the production of images and dreams. *Journal of Nervous and Mental Disease,* 174 (7), 397–407.

Katz, Y. Oct. 1965. Subliminal perception and the creative preconscious. *Dissertation Abstracts International,* 34 (4–B), 1751.

Key, W. 1974. *Subliminal Seduction.* New York: Signet.

Key, W. 1981. *Clam Plate Orgy.* New York: Signet.

Kilbourne, W. E.; Painton, S.; and Ridley, D. 1985. The effect of sexual embedding on responses to magazine advertisements. *Journal of Advertising,* 14 (2), 48–55.

Klein, G. S. 1956. Perception, motives and personality: A clinical perspective. In J. L. McCary, ed., *Psychology of Personality.* New York: Logos.

Klein, G. S. 1970. *Perception, Motives and Personality.* New York: Knopf.

Kostandov, E. A., and Arzumanov, IuL. May-June 1978. Conditioned reflex mechanism of unconscious decision making. *Zh Vyssh Nerv Deiat,* 28 (3), 542–8.

Kostandov, E. A.; Arzumanov, J.; Vazhnova, T.; Reschikova, T.; Shostakovich, G. Oct.-Dec. 1980. *Pavlov Journal of Biological Science,* 15 (4), 142–50.

Kostandov, E. A. 1977. Cortical evoked potentials to emotional words (supraliminal and subliminal). *Activities Nervosa Superior,* 19 (4), 301–2.

Kostandov, E. A., and Arzumanov, IuL. July 1986. The influence of subliminal emotional words on functional hemispheric asymmetry. *International Journal of Psychophysiology,* 4 (2), 143–47.

Kotulak, R. 8 May 1988. Mapping the learning and memory pathways of the brain. *Chicago Tribune.*

Krishnamurti, J. 1972. Lecture, Univ. of California at Berkeley.

Kwawer, J. S. Apr. 1972. An experimental study of psychoanalytic theories of overt male homosexuality. *Dissertation Abstracts International,* 32 (10–B), 6053.

Kwawer, J. S. Feb. 1977). Male homosexual psychodynamics and the Rorschach test. *Journal of Personal Assess,* 41 (1), 10–18.

Laing, R. 1967. *Politics of Experience.* New York: Ballantine Books Inc.

Lauprecht, C. May 1987. Unpublished lecture presented to Gormac Polygraph School in Ontario, California.

Leclerc, C., and Freibergs, V. Aug. 1971. The influence of perceptual and symbiotic subliminal stimuli on concept formation. *Canadian Journal of Psychology* (Canada), 25 (4), 292–301.

Ledford, B. R., and Ledford, S. Y. Nov. 1985. The effects of preconscious cues upon the automatic activation of self-esteem of selected middle school students. Requirement for Project 1246. Tucson Unified School District.

Ledford, B. P. Aug. 1978. The effects of thematic content of rheostatically controlled visual subliminals upon the receiving level of the affective domain of learners.

Lee, I., and Tyrer, P. Jan. 1980. Responses of chronic agoraphobics to subliminal and supraliminal phobic motion pictures. *Journal of Nervous and Mental Disease,* 168 (1), 34–40.

Lee, I.; Tyrer, P.; Horn, S. Oct. 1983. A comparison on subliminal, supraliminal and faded phobic cinefilms in the treatment of agoraphobia. *British Journal of Psychiatry,* 143, 356–61.

Libet, B.; Alberts, W. W.; and Wright, E. W. 1976. Responses of human somatosensory cortex to stimuli below threshold for conscious sensation. *Science,* 158 (3808), 1597–1600.

Lieberman, H. J. May 1975. A study of the relationship between developmentally determined personality and associated thought styles and tachistoscopic exposure time as reflected in conflict resolution. *Dissertation Abstracts International,* 35(11–B), 5670–71.

Linehan, E., and O'Toole, J. Mar. 1982. Effect of subliminal stimulation of symbiotic fantasies on college student self-disclosure in group counseling. *Journal of Counseling Psychology,* 29 (2), 151–57.

Litwack, T. R.; Wiedemann, C. F.; and Yager, J. Feb. 1979. The fear of object loss, responsiveness to subliminal stimuli, and schizophrenic psychopathology. *Journal of Nervous and Mental Disease,* 167 (2), 79–90.

Lofflin, J. 20 Mar. 1988. Help from the hidden persuaders. *New York Times.*

Lorenzo Gonzales, J. Jan.-Feb. 1985. Subliminal stimuli, unconscious psychopathological behavior, diagnostic and therapeutic implications. U Autonoma de Madrid, Facultad de Psicologia, Spain, 6 (1), 30–40.

Lukav. 1988. *World Goodwill Newletter,* no. 2. New York, New York.

177

Maltz, M. 1960. *Psychocybernetics.* New York: Simon and Schuster.

Mandel, K. H. May 1970. Problems and initiation of behavior therapy with male homosexuals. *Zeitschrift fur Psychotherapie und Medizinishe Psychologie,* 20 (3), 115–25.

Marcel, A. J. Apr. 1983. Conscious and unconscious perception: experiments on visual masking and word recognition. *Cognitive Psychology,* 15 (2), 197–237.

Marketing (Canada's Weekly Newspaper of Marketing Communications). 19 Jan. 1987, pp. 1, 3. CRTC changes mind on television rules.

Marketing Communications. Apr. 1985, p. 8. Subliminal testing: 25 years later.

Marketing News. 7 June 1985, pp. 7, 24. Outdoor advertising requires great use of creativity.

Marketing News. 15 Mar. 1985, pp. 5–6. Threshold messaging touted as antitheft measure.

McCormack, J. J. Dec. 1980. Effects of gender, intensity, and duration of sex-related visual subliminals upon the submission of controlled attention. *Dissertation Abstracts International,* 41 (6–A), 2409–10.

McLaughlin, M. 2 Feb. 1987. Subliminal tapes urge shoppers to heed the warning sounds of silence: 'Don't steal.' *New England Business,* 9 (2), 36–37.

Mendelsohn, E., and Silverman, L. H. 1982. Effects of stimulating psychodynamically relevant unconscious fantasies on schizophrenic psychopathology. *Schizophrenia Bulletin,* 8 (3), 532–47.

Merchandising. Dec. 1983, p. 42. Stimutech (E. Lansing, Michigan) launches Expando-Vision, a device that delivers subliminal messages via computer.

Meyers, H. G. Feb. 1982. The effects of a double bind induced by conflicting visual and auditory subliminal stimuli. *Dissertation Abstracts International,* 42 (8–B), 3432.

Miller, J. M. Aug. 1974. The effects of aggressive stimulation upon young adults who have experienced the death of a parent during childhood and adolescence. *Dissertation Abstracts International,* 35 (2–B), 1055–56.

MIS Week. 21 Apr. 1986, p. 36. Study claims office computer is used as management fink.

Murch, G. M. 1965. A set of conditions for a consistent recovery of a subliminal stimulus. *Journal of Applied Psychology* (U. S.), 49 (4), 257–60.

Murch, G. M. 1967. Aftereffects of subliminal stimulation as a function of the delay between stimulus presentation and reaction to it. *Zeitschrift Fur Experimentelle and Angewandte Psychologie,* 1 (3), 463–73.

Murch, G. M. 1967. Temporal gradients of responses to subliminal stimuli. *Psychological Record,* 17 (4), 483–91.

Mykel, N., and Daves, W. F. May 1979. Emergence of unreported stimuli into imagery as a function of laterality of presentation: A replication and extension of research by Henley and Dixon (1974). *British Journal Psychology,* 70 (2), 253–58.

Nelson, J. Messages hidden in music are being widely used to combat shoplifting—and much more. *National Enquirer,* 25.

News release. 1 Oct. 1985, pp. 1–4. Post-yuppies—are they turning into computer sneaks?

News release. Oct. 1984, pp. 1–4. Controversial 'brainwashing' and self-hypnosis software release to public.

Nicholson, H. E. Mar. 1980. The effect of contradictory subliminal stimuli and sensitization thereto upon viewers' perception of videotaped testimony. *Dissertation Abstracts International,* 40 (9–A), 4802.

Norcross, J. 1986. *Handbook of Eclectic Psychotherapy.* New York: Bruner/Mazel, Inc.

O'Grady, M. June 1977. Effect of subliminal pictorial stimulation on skin resistance. *Perceptual and Motor Skills,* 44 (3), 1051–56.

Ostrander, S., and Schroeder, L. 1970. *Psychic Discoveries Behind the Iron Curtain.* Englewood Cliffs, N.J.: Prentice-Hall, Inc.

Overbeeke, C. J. Feb. 1986. Changing the perception of behavioral properties by subliminal presentation. *Perceptual and Motor Skills,* 62 (1), 255–58.

O'Grady, M. June 1977. Effect of subliminal pictorial stimulation on skin resistance. *Perceptual and Motor Skills,* 44(3), 1051–56.

Packard, V. 1957. *Hidden Persuaders.* New York: Affiliated Publishers.

Pajurkova-Flannery, E. M. Oct. 1979. Subliminal perception in the context of functional hemispheric asymmetries. *Dissertation Abstracts International,* 40 (4–B), 1870.

179

Palmatier, J. R., and Bronstein, P. H. Dec. 1980. Effects of subliminal stimulation of symbiotic merging fantasies on behavioral treatment of smokers. *Journal of Mental and Nervous Disorders,* 168 (12), 15–20.

Palumbo, R., and Gillman, I. Dec. 1984. Effects of subliminal activation of Oedipal fantasies on competitive performance: A replication and extension. *Journal of Mental and Nervous Disorders,* 172 (12), 737–41.

Parker, K. A. Jan. 1982. Effects of subliminal symbiotic stimulation on academic performance: Further evidence on the adaptation-enhancing effects of oneness fantasies. *Journal of Counseling Psychology,* 29 (1), 19–28.

Peck, M. S. 1983. *People of the Lie.* New York: Simon and Schuster.

Pert, C. Spring 1987. Neuropeptides: The emotions and bodymind. *Noetic Sciences Review,* Sausalito, California 94965.

Pfanner, D. A. May 1983. Sensitivity to subliminal stimulation: An investigation of subject variables and conditions affecting psychodynamic and derivative recovery response. *Dissertation Abstracts International,* 43 (11–B), 3739.

Providence *Journal.* 18 Feb. 1986, Sec B, p. 1. Enter a quiet voice against shoplifting.

Rao, P. K., and Rao, K. R. Sept. 1982. Two studies of ESP and subliminal perception. *Journal of Parapsychology,* 46 (3), 285–207.

Roe, B. 31 July 1988. Letter to author.

Roney-Dougal, S. July-Aug. 1981. The interface between psi and subliminal perception. *Parapsychology Review,* 12 (4), 12–18.

Ruben. Mar. 1988, wk. 3. Predicasts.

Ross, W. D., and Kaplan, J.D. 1970. *The Pocket Aristotle.* New York: Washington Square Press.

Rudolph, J. R. Oct. 1970. Selective subliminal perception relative to approach/avoidance tendencies. *Dissertation Abstracts International,* 31 (4–A), 1695.

Rutstein, E. June 1971. The effects of aggressive stimulation of suicidal patients: an experimental study of the psychoanalytic theory of suicide. *Dissertation Abstracts International,* 31 (12–B), 7611.

Rutstein, E. H., and Goldberger, L. 1973. The effects of aggressive stimulation on suicidal patients: An experimental study of the psychoanalytic theory of suicide. *Psychoanalysis and Contemporary Science,* 2, 157–74.

Sackeim, H. A., and Packer, G. Dec. 1977. Hemisphericity, cognitive set, and susceptibility to subliminal perception. *Journal of Abnormal Psychology,* 86 (6), 624–30.

Schmidt, J. M. Nov. 1981. The effects of subliminally present anaclitic and introjective stimuli on normal young adults. *Dissertation Abstracts International,* 42 (5–B), 2081.

Schurtman, R.; Palmatier, J. R.; and Martin, E. S. Oct. 1982. On the activation of symbiotic gratification fantasies as an aid in the treatment of alcoholics. *International Journal of Addiction,* 17 (7), 1157–74.

Shevrin, H., and Fisher, C. 1967. Changes in the effects of awaking subliminal stimulus as a function of dreaming and nondreaming sleep. *Journal of Abnormal Psychology,* 72 (4), 362–68.

Shevrin, H., and Rennick, P. 1967. Cortical responses to tactile during attention, mental arithmetic and free association. *Psychophysiology,* 3, 381–88.

Shevrin, H.; Smith, W. H.; and Hoobler, R. 1970. Direct measurement of unconscious mental process: Average evoked response and free association correlates of subliminal stimulation. *Psychological Association,* 5 (Pt. 2), 543–44.

Shevrin, H.; Smith, W. H.; and Fritzler, D. E. 1969. Repressiveness as a factor in the subliminal activation of brain and verbal responses. *Journal of Nervous and Mental Disease,* 149 (3), 2261–69.

Shevrin, H.; Smith, W. H.; and Fritzler, D. E. 1970. Subliminally stimulated brain and verbal responses of twins differing in repressiveness. *Journal of Abnormal Psychology,* 76 (1), 39–46.

Shevrin, H., and Fritzler, D. E. 1968. Visual evoked response correlates of unconscious mental processes. *Science,* 161 (3838), 295–98.

Shifren, I. W. Apr. 1982. The interaction between hemispheric preference and the perception of subliminal auditory and visual symbiotic gratification stimuli. *Dissertation Abstracts International,* 42 (10–B), 4211,12.

Silbert, J. Aug. 1982. Human symbiosis, the holding environment and schizophrenia: An experimental study. *Dissertation Abstracts International,* 43 (2–B), 535.

181

Silverman, L. H.; Linger, H.; Lustbader, L.; Farrell, J.; and Martin, A. D. June 1972. Effects of subliminal drive stimulation on the speech of stutterers. *Journal of Nervous and Mental Disease* (U. S.), 155 (1), 14–21.

Silverman, L. H. Dec. 1975. An experimental method for the study of unconscious conflict: A progressive report. *British Journal of Medical Psychology,* 8 (4), 291–98.

Silverman, L. H.; Kwawer, J. S.; Wolitzky, C.; and Coron, M. Aug. 1973. An experimental study of aspects of the psychoanalytic theory of male homosexuality. *Journal of Abnormal Psychology* (U.S.), 82 (1), 178–89.

Silverman, L. H. Mar. 1971. An experimental technique for the study of unconscious conflict. *British Journal of Medical Psychology,* 44 (1), 17–25.

Silverman, L. H. Jan. 1970. Further experimental studies of dynamic propositions in psychoanalysis: On the function and meaning of regressive thinking. *Journal of the American Psychoanalytic Association,* 18 (1), 102–24.

Silverman, L. H.; Bronstein, A.; and Mendelsohn, E. Spring 1976. The further use of the subliminal psychodynamic activation method for the experimental study of the clinical theory of psychoanalysis: On the specificity of the relationship between symptoms and unconscious. *Psychotherapy: Theory, Research and Practice,* 13 (1), 2–16.

Silverman, L. H. 1975. On the role of laboratory experiments in the development of the clinical theory of psychoanalysis: Data on the subliminal activation of aggressive and merging wishes in schizophrenics. *International Review of Psycho-Analysis,* 2 (1), 43–64.

Silverman, L. H.; Frank, S. G.; and Dachinger, P. June 1974. A psychoanalytic reinterpretation of the effectiveness of systematic desensitization: Experimental data bearing on the role of merging fantasies. *Journal of Abnormal Psychology,* 83 (3), 313–18.

Silverman, L. H. Sept. 1976. Psychoanalytic theory: "The reports of my death are greatly exaggerated." *American Psychologist,* 31 (9), 621–37.

Silverman, L. H.; Ross, D. L.; Adler, J. M.; and Lustig, D. A. June 1978. Simple research paradigm for demonstrating subliminal psychodynamic activation: effects of oedipal stimulation on dart-throwing accuracy in college males. *Journal of Abnormal Psychology,* 87 (3), 341–57.

Silverman, L. H.; Martin, A.; Ungaro, R.; and Mendelsohn, E. 1978. Effect of subliminal stimulation of symbiotic fantasies on behavior modification treatment of obesity. *Journal of Consulting and Clinical Psychology,* 46, 432–41.

Singh, Y., and Devi, R. M. Jan.-July 1976. Subliminal guessing: A communication of collegiate students. *Psycho-Lingua,* 6 (1–2), 23–28.

Slipp, S., and Nissenfeld, S. Oct. 1981. An experimental study of psychoanalytic theories of depression. *Journal of American Academic Psychoanalysis,* 9 (4), 583–600.

Smith, G. J.; Gudmund, J.; and Carlsson, I. Spring 1986. Creativity and aggression. *Psychoanalytic Psychology,* 3 (2), 159–72.

Smith, G. J., and Carlsson, I. 1983. Creativity and anxiety: An experimental study. *Scandinavian Journal of Psychology,* 24 (2), 107–15.

Smith, G. J.; Gudmund, J.; Carlsson, I.; and Danielsson, A. 1985. Identification with another person: Manipulated by means of subliminal stimulation. *Scandinavian Journal of Psychology,* 26 (1), 74–87.

Smith, G. J., and Danielsson, A. 1979. The influence of anxiety on the urge for aesthetic creation: An experimental study utilizing subliminal stimulation and a percept-genetic technique. *Psychological Research Bulletin,* Lund Univ., 19 (3–4), 36.

Smith, G. J., and Danielsson, A. 1979. A test of identification using subliminal stimulation in a metacontrast design: Preliminary validation with sensitive-paranoid and borderline subjects. *Psychological Research Bulletin,* Lund Univ., 19 (9–10),23.

Soininen, K., and Jarvilehto, T. Nov. 1983. Somatosensory evoked potentials associated with tactile stimulation at detection threshold in man. *Electroencephalogr Clinical Neurophysiology,* 56 (5), 494–500.

Somekh, D. E. Nov. 1976. The effect of embedded words in a brief visual display. *British Journal of Psychology,* 67 (4), 529–35.

Somekh, D. E., and Wilding, J. M. Aug. 1973. Perception without awareness in a dichoptic viewing situation. *British Journal of Psychology,* 64 (3), 339–49.

183

Sommer, L. Mar. 1986. The effects of subliminal psychodynamic activation on verbal time estimation. *Dissertation Abstracts International,* 46 (9–B), 3231.

South Ogden Police Department. 1987. Ogden, Utah.

Spence, D. P. 1983. Subliminal effects on lexical decision time. *Archiv fur Psychologie,* 135 (1), 67–72.

Spence, D. P. 1967. Subliminal perception and perceptual defense: 2 sides of a single problem. *Behavioral Science,* 12 (3), 183–93.

Spence, D. 1981. *Psychological Research Bulletin,* Lund Univ., 21 (7), 7.

Steinberg, R. J. Oct. 1975. The effects of subliminal mother- need tachistoscopic stimulation on the ego pathology of hospitalized male schizophrenics. *Dissertation Abstracts International,* 36 (4–B), 1934.

Strauch, I., et al. 1976. The impact of meaningful auditory signals on sleeping behavior. *Archiv fur Psychologie,* 128 (1–2), 75–95.

Sturman, P. A. July 1980. Derivatives of the castration complex in normal adults. *Dissertation Abstracts International* 41 (1–B), 370.

Taylor, E. 1986. *Subliminal Communication: Emperor's Clothes or Panacea?* Salt Lake City: Just Another Reality Publishing.

Taylor, E. 1987. *Subliminal Technology.* Salt Lake City: PAR, Inc.

Tripe, B. Validity in subliminal messages? Professionals tend to disagree. United Press International.

Tuthill, P. 1988. *The 100,000 Message Hoax?* Catalog of Consumer Alert, Mind Communications, Grand Rapids, Michigan.

Tyrer, P.; Lewis, P.; and Lee, I. Feb. 1978. Effects of subliminal and supraliminal stress on symptoms of anxiety. *Journal of Nervous and Mental Disease,* 166 (2), 88–95.

Tyrer, P.; Horn, S.; and Lee, I. Feb. 1978. Treatment of agoraphobia by subliminal and supraliminal exposure to phobiccine film. *Lancet,* 1 (8060), 358–60.

Valind, B., and Valind, L. 1968. Effects of subliminal stimulation on homographs. *Psychological Research Bulletin,* 88, 89.

VandenBoogert, C. 1984. A study of potentials unlimited subliminal persuasion/self-hypnosis tapes. Potentials Unlimited, Inc., Grand Rapids, Michigan.

Varga, M. P. Feb. 1974. An experimental study of aspects of the psychoanalytic theory of elation. *Dissertation Abstracts International,* 34 (8–B), 4062–63.

VideoNews. 22 July 1983, pp. 4–5. Environmental video has introduced a subliminal persuasion videocassette that superimposes low-level video messages on cassette tapes.

Vokey, J. R., and Read, J. D. Nov. 1985. Subliminal messages: Between the devil and the media. *American Psychology,* 40 (11), 1231–39.

Voronin, L. G.; Novikov, P. P.; Volkov, E. V.; and Dubynin, V. A. Sept.-Oct. 1984. Formation and development of temporary connections with participation of unconscious and conscious stimuli. *Zh Vyssh Nerv Deiat,* 34 (5), 855–60.

Wagstaff, G. F. Aug. 1974. The effects of repression- sensitization of a brightness scaling measure of perceptual defence. *British Journal of Psychology,* 65 (3), 395–401.

Walker, P. Aug. 1975. The subliminal perception of movement and the 'supression' in binocular rivalry. *British Journal of Psychology,* 66 pt 3, 347–56.

Wall Street Journal. 3 Star, Eastern (Princeton, NJ) Edition. 5 June 1985), p. 33. Canadian radio station broadcasting 'anti- mosquito' frequencies.

Watson, G. B. 1970. Motor response latency as an indicator of subliminal affective stimulation. *Journal of General Psychology,* 82 (2), 139–43.

Watson, J. P. Dec. 1975. An experimental method for the study of unconscious conflict. *British Journal of Medical Psychology,* 49 (4), 299–301.

Wechsler, R. Feb. 1987. A new prescription: Mind over malady. *Discover Magazine.*

Westerlundh, B. 1983. The motives of defence: Perceptogenetic studies: I. Shame. *Psychological Research Bulletin,* Lund Univ., 23 (7), 13.

Wilbur, K. 1982. *The Holographic Paradigm and Other Paradoxes.* Boulder, Colorado: New Science Library.

Williams, L. J., and Evans, J. R. Feb. 1980. Evidence for perceptual defense using a lexical decision task. *Perceptual Motor Skills,* 50 (1), 195–98.

Wolman, B. B., ed. 1973. *Handbook of General Psychology.* Englewood Cliffs, N.J.: Prentice-Hall.

Women's Wear Daily. Mar. 1987, p. 30. Pier Auge's reentry more exclusive.

Zanot, E. J.; Pincus, J. D.; and Lamp, E. J. 1983. Public perceptions of subliminal advertising. *Journal of Advertising,* 12 (1), 39–45.

Zanot, E. J., and Maddox, L. M. July 1983. Subliminal advertising and education. Paper presented at the Annual meeting of the Association for Education in Journalism (65th, Athens, Ohio, July 25–28, 1982).

Zenhausern, R., and Hansen, K. Apr. 1974. Differential effect of subliminal and supraliminal accessory stimulation on task components in problem-solving. *Perceptual and Motor Skills* (U. S.), 39 (2), 375.

Zenhausern, R.; Pompo, C.; and Ciaiola, M. Apr. 1974. Simple and complex reaction time as a function of subliminal and supraliminal accessory stimulation. *Perceptual and Motor Skills* (U. S.), 38 (2), 417–18.

Zenhausern, R.; Ciaiola, M.; and Pompo, C. Aug. 1973. Subliminal and supraliminal accessory stimulation and two trapezoid illusions. *Perceptual and Motor Skills,* 37 (19), 251–56.

Zuckerman, S. G. June 1981. An experimental study of underachievement: The effects of subliminal merging and success-related stimuli on the academic performance of bright underachieving high school students. *Dissertation Abstracts International,* 41 (12–B), 4699–4700.

Zukov, G. 1980. *The Dancing Wuli Waters.* London: Collins.

Zwosta, M. F., and Zenhausern, R. June 1969. Application of signal detection theory to subliminal and supraliminal accessory stimulation. *Perceptual and Motor Skills* (U. S.), 28 (3), 699–70.

Index

83625